The Holiday Makers

*Understanding the impact
of leisure and tourism*

JOST KRIPPENDORF

Translated by Vera Andrassy

BUTTERWORTH
HEINEMANN

OXFORD   AMSTERDAM   BOSTON   LONDON   NEW YORK   PARIS
SAN DIEGO   SAN FRANCISCO   SINGAPORE   SYDNEY   TOKYO

Butterworth-Heinemann
An imprint of Elsevier Science
Linacre House, Jordan Hill, Oxford OX2 8DP
225 Wildwood Avenue, Woburn MA 01801-2041

First published in Great Britain 1987
Reprinted as a paperback edition 1989
Reprinted 1990, 1991, 1992, 1994, 1997
Reissued with a new cover 1999
Transferred to digital printing 2002

British Library Cataloguing in Publication Data
A catalogue record for this book is available from the British Library

ISBN 0 7506 4348 X

For information on all Butterworth-Heinemann Publications
visit our website at www.bh.com

Printed and bound in Great Britain by Antony Rowe Ltd, Eastbourne

Contents

Preface

When I tell people that thinking about leisure and tourism is my profession, they often smile. Obviously, they do not find it serious, they do not see it as work, and only work can be serious. At these moments I almost always feel I should apologize. Of course, they say, leisure and travel are perhaps two of the nicest things in the world, but really, when you get down to it, they are rather trivial matters. I believe they are much more than that, for they concern the happiness of the individual and the well-being of our society, and these, everyone would agree, are central issues in our lives. Leisure and holidays should not be reduced to something that one can leave without further ado to the entertainment industry. For many years people fought for more leisure time and holidays for everyone. Today we have to fight the effects of their success. In my view what we have failed to do is develop forms of travel that are psychologically, socially, economically and ecologically compatible.

Almost ten years have passed between my book *The Landscape Eaters* and the now published *The Holiday Makers* – a long gap, but one I needed for thinking and getting the necessary detachment from the field I was writing about. While the mid-seventies saw a growing interest in the impact of tourism on the environment, today, when travel has become a mass phenomenon unequalled in history, people are beginning to discover the human dimension and the socio-cultural problems linked with leisure time mobility. This interest should have started much earlier. Indeed, this is where it should have all begun.

Here, then, are two books that try to express the spirit of the age. Neither of them contains anything which was unknown before, they are, rather, a compilation of existing knowledge from many sources. Part of the material has come from the grey zones of scientific or technical books and libraries and then translated into everyday speech. Some of it consists of my own ideas and experiences. What

I have concerned myself with, has been, above all, the establishment of relationships. The 'new' as the result of an overall view of
things.

What I have presented is certainly not always free from contradictions – they cannot be avoided, life is too full of them. Nor have I
always succeeded in solving all my uncertainties and doubts. Thus, I
am hereby presenting them for evaluation and criticism. I write in
order to get a step further myself and perhaps set some things in
motion; certainly to set a discussion going.

As an economist trained in only one discipline – which, by the way, is
how economists are still, quite inadequately, trained in most universi-
ties – I had to venture into many areas of knowledge that were new to
me, above all sociology, psychology and pedagogy. It was not all plain
sailing. May the specialists therefore have some forbearance and turn a
blind eye to my lumberings. My spiritual borrowings – always duly
recognized and quoted – have, above all, been taken from four persons
with whom I have been linked by friendly and professional ties for
many years now. They are:

Pierre Lainé, sociologist and economist, founder of 'Renouveau', a
national association for holidays, leisure time and culture in Chambéry
and Paris; Paul Rieger, Evangelist theologian and holiday psychologist,
founder and chairman of the study circle for tourism in Starnberg,
Federal Republic of Germany; Roman Bleistein, Catholic theologian,
professor of pedagogy at the School of Philosophy, Munich; Horst
Opaschowski, professor of leisure time pedagogy at Hamburg
University and head of the BAT-Leisure Time-Research Institute in
Hamburg.

All four of them have written about aspects of leisure and travel
which I find important. I hope I have not betrayed their ideas but
perhaps even developed them a step further.

My warm thanks go to my collaborators Bernhard Kramer, Ralph
Krebs and Hansruedi Müller for examining ·and evaluating the
comprehensive literature, collecting the photo material and not least
for their many valuable suggestions.

I should like to express my special thanks to the Swiss Hotel
Association and the Swiss Travel Saving Fund. Their generous
financial support to a research project 'New Developments in Leisure
and Their Effects on Tourism' has enabled my Institute to expand the
area of its studies, the first result of which is the present book.

I should like to dedicate my book to all those who would like to
think about their role as holiday-makers or about their task in the

leisure and travel world of tomorrow. I hope there are many of them.

Jost Krippendorf
Berne, May 1987

Introduction

You need a change of soul rather than a change
of climate. You must lay aside the burdens of the
mind; until you do this, no place will satisfy you.
Seneca

Masses on the move

A restless activity has taken hold of the once so sedentary human
society. Most people in the industrialized countries have been seized by
a feverish desire to move. Every opportunity is used to get away from
the workday routine as often as possible. Shorter trips during the week
and on weekends, longer journeys during the holidays. The fondest
wish for old age is a new place to which to retire. Anything to get away
from home! Away from here, at any cost!

Thus, year in year out, weekend after weekend, without any real
necessity and without overt pressure, millions of people flock
together to spend their precious free time. They all participate in
it of their own free will, and yet as if following orders. They form
long lines of cars or get transported in bus, jumbo jet and train
shipments. They lie crammed together on beaches that have become
too small. They queue up in shops and restaurants, for ski lifts and
cable cars and before not-to-be-missed sights, worn out from
centuries of being admired. Sometimes they stay in accommodation
reminiscent of slums. If employees were subjected to such stress
during their working hours, according to one behaviour researcher,
trade unions and medical officers would quite rightly intervene.[1*]
Compared to the amount of travelling done today in leisure time,
the migrations of peoples in Antiquity look like modest works
outings!

* References are collected in a section beginning on page 149.

Come to think of it, we should, in fact, be happy that something that
had for so many years been the pleasure of a small minority has now
developed into a sport for the masses: mobility, holidays, travel as a
social achievement. But somehow the joy of it is slow in setting in. The
thing has a seamy side for we have had to pay for what we have
achieved – we have had to give something in return. The effects of our
mobility, of the new freedom we fought so hard to win, threaten to
engulf us. The questions that now emerge are whether, in the final
analysis, we have gained something or lost something and how things
are supposed to go on from here.

What has led to this leisure mobility, which has become a factor that
determines the lives of many townspeople and on which they spend
about 40 per cent of their spare time? 30 per cent of this time is used up
on trips and short journeys, 10 per cent on longer holiday travel.[2] And
yet, man was not born a tourist. True, a yearning for far-away places
and curiosity have always belonged to his inborn and strongly felt
urges. They were one of the motives behind the elegant travel of the
upper classes until the beginning of this century. But what drives
millions of people from their homes today is not so much an innate
need to travel. If we observe how people travel, what they do during
their holidays and what they chiefly talk about, we shall easily discover
that the drive to explore new things and learn something new, plays a
very small part in it.

The travel needs of the modern age have been largely created by
society and shaped by everyday life. People go away because they no
longer feel happy where they are – where they work, where they live. In
order to be able to carry on, they urgently need a temporary refuge
from the burdens imposed by the everyday work, home and leisure
scene. Their work is increasingly automated and functionalized; it is
also determined by other people. They feel the monotony of the daily
routine, the cold rationality of factories, offices, apartment blocks and
transport, shrinking human contact, the repression of feelings, the loss
of nature and naturalness. For many people these are part of the
disadvantages of everyday living – they feel that life has been reduced
to mere existence. It leads to stress, physical and mental exhaustion,
emptiness and boredom. In order to redress the imbalance, to find what
we miss or have lost in everyday life, we go away: the aim is to switch
off and fill up, enjoy the independence, make our own decisions, find
new friends, have a break, feel free and take home some happiness and
memories. In fact, we travel in order to live and survive. The great
departures of the masses in today's modern age is a consequence of

circumstances, bestowed upon us by the development of industrial society.

But that society has given its members not only the motives but also the means of escaping: money, in the form of higher incomes, and time, thanks to ever shorter working hours and longer holidays. What is most important, industry has developed for us a vehicle which has really set the 'auto-mobile' society going. The car, and to a somewhat lesser extent the aeroplane, have ushered in the mobile leisure revolution and brought it at breakneck speed, in a period of about two decades, to what it is today. All predictions concur: those who are not mobile today, will become mobile in the very near future. Free driving for free people! The car as a symbol of freedom par excellence. One could almost speak of a general claim to individual motorization and limitless individual mobility that we think is ours by natural right.

After all, society has placed the leisure industry at our disposal as a kind of friend and helper. It has taken charge of our leisure time and offers not only fulfilment but produces, where necessary, the corresponding desires and yearnings. Leisure and holidays as a contrasting programme to the industrial world have themselves become an industry. It is the business of the twentieth century!

All this falls into a kind of cycle, which may be termed the recreation cycle of man within industrial society: we travel in order to recharge the batteries, to restore our physical and mental strength. On our trip we consume the climate, nature and landscapes, the culture and people in the places we visit, which become 'therapy zones' for the purpose. We then return home, more or less fit, to defy everyday life until next time. The trick has worked! But the wish to leave again and even more often is soon with us again, because life cannot be made up for in a few weeks of holidays and on weekends. The waggon is overloaded, it overflows with wishes and longings. It is this continuous repetition of unrealized and unrealizable needs that gives the cycle its dynamics. We work in order to go on holiday, among other things, and we need the holidays in order to be able to work again. We temporarily free ourselves of the harness only to have it put on again even tighter. If there were no escape-aid – tourism – clinics and sanatoria would have to be built to cure people from the stress of the workaday routine. Tourism is social therapy, the valve that maintains the world in good running order! It has a stabilizing effect not only on the individual but on our entire society and its economy. Sociologists have proved it:[3] once people have succeeded in changing the scene, in switching off, they develop the need to exchange the transitoriness of tourism for the soothing stability of everyday life. People travel so that they may be confirmed in the belief that home is not so bad after all, indeed that it is perhaps the best of all. They travel in order to return. The economy too needs tourism as an energy producer for the regeneration of the work force. This is certainly not the least of the reasons why we have been granted more leisure time.

This, then, is roughly how the great recreation machine works. A cycle repeated year in year out and in which we are all involved without being aware of it.

Mass migration encounters limits

But of late sand has entered the wheels of this enormous machine. What seemed to function without a hitch is still running but now not quite so smoothly. On many sides the question has been raised about the purpose of the whole thing and where it is taking us. There are growing indications that the massive flight from towns, which is the present pattern of tourism, cannot be a long lasting therapy; that the thing has no future in its current form. But many people are still happily unconcerned and blissfully assume it will all continue according to the slogan: more, bigger, faster, further. It is true that most forecasts support their conviction, especially traffic forecasts, because traffic can obviously only increase. And the often quoted statement of a well-known American futurologist, saying that in the year 2000 the travel industry will be the world's biggest, is also grist to their mill.[4]

But shouldn't we be a bit more sceptical and ask ourselves a few questions? If we do, we will realize that the future is no longer what it used to be – that it no longer consists of an estimable and manageable expansion and that we can certainly no longer assume that everything will go on as before. Many new signals all point to a change of course.

More and more people are beginning to notice that something must be wrong with the system. The serious shortcomings felt in everyday life cannot be offset by a few brief moments of freedom, of creative inspiration, of happiness and self-determination during leisure and holiday time. They are no longer satisfied with ersatz freedom, with life in bits and pieces. They demand, openly or secretly, more life altogether. Already ten years ago there was the following little poem in a school reader:[5]

> With time
> you no longer
> want to dream
> the whole day about evening,
> the whole week
> about Friday,
> the whole year about holidays.
> With time
> you no longer
> want to dream
> about a new life
> which is only
> half a life.

A joyless society should develop into a joyful one. For an increasing number of people work is no longer the main purpose in life, and uneasiness about the present state of affairs and the wish to change something are becoming more and more widespread. What is it though, that should be changed and to what extent?

Another serious question for the future is the crisis that has spread to most industrialized countries: working society seems to be gradually running out of work. How can we cope with this new situation?

Then there are the ecologists and conservationists, who also want things to change. They want to get at the tourist landscape-eaters that are at work everywhere. For example, they will try to prevent the building of second homes in the countryside, which, according to forecasts, will soon equal one-third of all building in big towns. They want to bring to a halt the impetuous expansion of the road network, prompted above all by the increase in leisure traffic. They will also oppose the furnishing of our recreation areas with all kinds of leisure facilities. They, who used to be kind of shadow organization, the green mafia, have developed into a powerful movement, and are gaining support. What will be the outcome of their struggle?

Sensitivity to the negative effects of the tourist mass migration is also beginning to develop in the local population in the tourist areas. There is a growing feeling of being literally overrun and squeezed out by tourists. Don't we occasionally get the impression that local people are fed up with tourism? They want to shake off the dictatorship of the trade, take their destiny into their own hands, make their own decisions and participate in their development. What they want above all else is to shape their own environment as a place for themselves and not as a playground for other people. The locals are getting near to rebellion. True, they are (still) doing all they can to attract tourists, but they would, equally, like to do their best to prevent them from coming. It would seem, then, that a ceiling has been reached here, one of a psychological nature.

'. . . *Or else we must change the system*'

We want to examine these and other questions in the hope of arriving at something that could be more desirable than what we have today. In this we do not intend to pronounce a sweeping condemnation on all that has been created and achieved so far. Even less do we want to turn modern tourism into a scapegoat and use it in unadvised social criticism. All those who describe the exodus of millions as the greatest plague of the western world, as the decline of civilization, as mass deception or even as a repressive instrument which our society uses to maintain a freedomless situation, as 'opium for the people' and call for its abolition, these people make the game too easy for themselves.[6] They are engaging in futile criticism of a phenomenon that has long since become measurable reality and an extremely important social, economic and political factor. No matter how brilliant their essays or comments, the facts on which they are based are scanty. The massive flight from towns we mentioned earlier is not a carefully planned and devilish scheme of capitalist slave-drivers and wire-pullers. It is quite simply another aspect of the development of our industrial society – the reverse side of the coin, as its critics would say. But let us not forget: this same industrial society has brought us real social achievements and progress. It has freed us from the terrible pressure of poverty. It has provided us with a roof over our heads and supplied durable means for the satisfaction of our basic needs. Over and above that, it has given us many things we would not like to do without. We have been able to improve significantly our personal situation, our living standards – and we have worked hard for it. What we have achieved is a fact and cannot be eliminated from the world. It must be accepted and recognized as such. Of course, criticism of the system from the safe shelter of existing achievements is all too easy, but when development begins to bring the individual and society more disadvantages than advantages, there comes a time when criticism, and above all reflection, must take their cue. That time has now come. Our economic system, based on the merry-go-round of production and consumption, consumption and production, has developed a dangerous dynamics of its own. It is no longer a question of satisfying real human needs. Most of these have been satisfied. Nor is it a question of creating new values. The economy has moved away from people. It has placed itself above them and made itself independent in a way. It works in order to maintain its own apparatus and perpetuate itself. For this purpose it has created an alibi called force of circumstances. And force creates fear. A careful look around will show us that in many areas the cost to society, the economy and the environment by far exceeds the benefits derived from so-called development. Here is just one example: in most tourist areas and resorts a real estate market has grown up which follows its own laws and which has completely disassociated itself from tourism. The sale of building land, the building of new chalets, holiday flats, apartment blocks, hotels and other structures is still in full swing. All this is going on despite the fact that occupancy rates in existing facilities are, for the most part, disappointingly low and declining every year, and landscapes are losing more and more of their recreational quality. It is no secret that the construction lobby is especially efficient. It would have us believe that its activities are justified by force of circumstances: namely, preservation of jobs in the building industry.

Analysing this situation, one leisure time researcher recently put it like this:[7] mass tourism is one of the most marked, most momentous and least manageable forms of the leisure shock. We believe we have learned how to live with it. We live under the illusion that we can dam its excesses, foresee its development, eliminate its weaknesses. But in reality all we can do is wait and see what ecological, psychological and socio-economic consequences mass tourism will yet produce. Either that, or we must change our approach, change the system, produce new assumptions.

This is exactly what we should be concerned with today: we must try to see where the existing system has failed; where the ground of reality has become barren, the very ground to which people who develop new ideas are told by their critics to return to! We must learn to understand that the mere continuation of present economic and technical trends cannot bring us what we really desire in the future. Indeed, such a development would be the most inadequate, shabbiest and dangerous of all possible futures! But haven't we become so enslaved by the force of circumstances that we no longer even dare think about what we really want?[8]

Should we decide to tackle the problem, we must transcend the established intellectual framework and base our decisions on entirely new criteria. Theories, economic estimates, political programmes and doctrines will not take us very far. Moreover, and above all, we need intuition and imagination; social imagination or the ability not to accept the existing situation as something final. We need to create something different and formulate an alternative to the current state of affairs.

As we have already observed, leisure, and tourism as one of its forms, are not worlds in themselves, following their own laws. They are the results and at the same time integral parts of industrial society and its organization. Clearly then, leisure activities have an impact on the system and cannot be understood if they are isolated from their original determining factors. Modern tourism is one of the most striking and strangest phenomena of our times. The only way to probe its nature is to try to understand how things are connected, and to distinguish between cause and effect, expectation and reality. It is only when we realize how the mechanism works that we can learn to control it, change it and improve it.

And yet, these relationships cannot be identified if they are viewed from a narrow, monodisciplinary angle. If once we broaden our horizons, we shall see that suddenly everything becomes relevant and exerts some influence. The subject becomes broader and broader: work, home, leisure time and life in general must all be taken into account. It makes us wonder about the nature of progress and about what we ourselves consider as desirable, about our own position. And this train of thought brings us back to our original subject: leisure time and travel.

In the first, shorter part of my book I shall try to sketch a rough outline of the life model consisting of work – home – free time – travel. This will provide the general framework for our subject. In the second part of the book I shall describe the processes that determine our free time and, within that, our mobility. I want to take a close look at what I have described as the recreation cycle of man in industrial society; namely travel in its current form. With all its blessings, but also with its vicissitudes and unfulfilled promises, and, above all, with its trends and prospects. In the third part of my book, I ask whether there exist new tendencies which may perhaps change everything: the everyday world, the economy, work, home life, and leisure time; people's attitudes and the ideals of our society. Are we not surrounded by developments which, if given our support, could make everyday life more humane, and as a consequence of which the quality of travel could also improve? In the last part of the book I have included proposals for the humanization of travel, appealing for a new understanding of this and of leisure. Such an approach holds a great deal of promise, because we certainly do not want to abolish holidays and travel. On the contrary. But we must develop such forms of leisure which will bring all those involved as much benefit as possible but not at the expense of other people or of the environment. Indeed, holidays and outdoor recreation could perhaps become a field of learning and experimentation for everyday life. Then we would not travel to forget everyday life, to find a diversion from the everyday situation which no longer satisfies us, but in order to realize that there is a chance. The chance to gain something, to practise freedom, mutual understanding and solidarity and to save a piece of it for everyday life. It is here that we shall find the answer to the delicate question whether it is morally defensible to be concerned with the recreational needs of people in industrialized countries, while millions of people in other parts of the world must struggle daily for mere survival. A new understanding of travel and the adoption of different attitudes and behaviour while travelling may help to develop our sense for greater humanity and justice. Tourism, then, as human enrichment, as a driving force for a better life in general, for a better society? Well, why not? It is this positive utopia, this ideal, for which we want to strive. For this purpose we should like to stimulate as much awareness as possible not only by demonstrating the interactions in the system but also by suggesting ways in which every individual can contribute in bringing us closer to the desired situation.

All this is not possible without raising critical questions and being quite explicit about our fears and apprehensions. It is not the well poisoner who will tell us that our wells have been poisoned. Criticism is not aimed at dismantling the system. Its purpose is to illuminate the paths that may lead out of the thicket: the roads to a better future. We cannot always produce scientific proof for what is presented here. Where data are missing – and that is often the case – we must rely on our own value judgements – on the way we personally would like things to be. And, by the way, when we are dealing with the future, no proofs can be demanded. They are certainly never required from those people who want the present situation to continue as it is, so why should those who propose changes be treated differently?

The desire to change something and try out something new is very strong in many people, perhaps stronger than ever before. So, let us join Ernst Bloch in his 'principle of hope'[9] – it consists in believing in the gentle force of consciousness, which becomes material force as soon as it reaches the masses – if the masses avail themselves of it.

PART ONE

The model of life in industrial society
Work – Home – Free Time – Travel

Since the Renaissance we have been constantly trying to go beyond our limits. Today we are trying to determine those limits. We have in fact reached the point where we have to ask, what lies beyond these newly identified limits.

Erhard Eppler

This is precisely *the* question of the century.

Michael Ende

I

An outline of the model

At the beginning of this book I shall try to put the subject of leisure and travel in a broader perspective. I shall also immediately outline my standpoint, show from what angle I am presenting my arguments, what my philosophy of life is, what I believe the social system we should be striving for looks like and thus lay my cards on the table so that everything is clear from the very outset. This will make it easier to understand what I am writing about. Figure 1 will serve as a skeleton for our purposes.

This diagram presents a kind of overall system. Its centre represents the focal point of our considerations: the recreation cycle of man in industrial society. The cycle begins with man and the spheres of everyday life – work, home and free time. Part of the free time is mobile leisure spent in travelling. This serves as an outlet or break from everyday life and is itself characterized by particular influences, motives and expectations. The tourist destination form the other pole. They represent what we shall call counter-everyday life or counter-routine. Of especial interest here is the behaviour and experience of travellers, the situation of the host population and their environment and the encounter between the visitors and the locals. Finally, tourism has an impact on, as well as repercussions for, the country and people of the host areas and for the situation at home. This pendulum movement between everyday life and counter-routine with its manifold interactions is the main theme of our book.

The structure: work – home – free time – travel is embedded in a broader framework and it is from there that it is shaped and influenced. In that framework four forces are operating, connected by a complex network of interactions. Those forces are:[1] society with its values (the socio-cultural sub-system); the economy and its structure (the economic sub-system); the environment and its resources (the ecological sub-system); the state and its policies (the political sub-system). Taken as a whole, these sub-systems represent the stage on which our life is set. Figure 1 shows the general direction in developments and trends in these four spheres during the past thirty years or so.

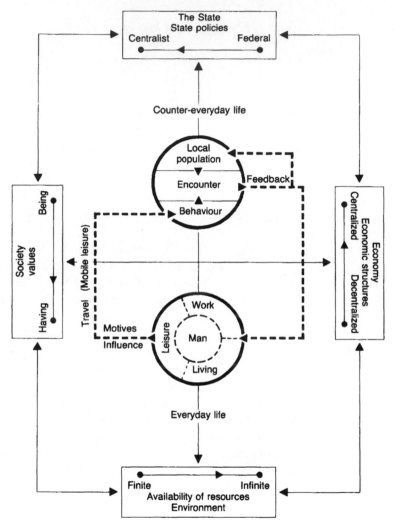

Figure 1   *The model of life in industrial society: work – home – free time – travel.*

In our society the values of 'being' have been superseded by those of 'having': possession, property, wealth, consumption and egoism have taken precedence over community, tolerance, moderation, sensibility, modesty, honesty.

The economy is characterized by growing control of business in the hands of a few; by an increase, that is in the number of huge consortiums with more and more economic power at the cost of independent small- and medium-sized businesses, which are now struggling for survival. There is also increasing division of labour and specialization together with rapidly disappearing self-sufficiency.

The environment is being treated and used as if resources were inexhaustible. Science and technology are continually providing new means of stretching the limits of the ecosystem; that is, of how much waste can be dumped back into the earth. This creates the illusion that the negative side-effects of economic growth can always be overcome and eliminated by modern technology.[2]

Lastly, there is no industrialized country in which state bureaucracy, the scope of state interests and expenditure – and consequently the tendency to more centralism in government – have not increased. The state is forced to develop an increasingly expensive infrastructure for the growing economic apparatus (transport, supply, public utilities), provide for regularity mechanisms ('booster injections', subsidies for 'lame-duck' industries) and ensure the smooth functioning of the growing economy. Public services must also be continually expanded: health care, education, help for fringe groups, protection of the threatened environment. All of these are indispensable services which only the state can provide.[3]

Even this brief description of the framework in which our lives are set will show us that many important aspects of the system are missing from the diagram: the system does not function as harmoniously as the diagram would have us believe. In reality the elements do not have such equal weight or status as they do on paper and each has to be measured by a different yardstick. The dominant ones exist at the expense of those given less importance. Instead of being complementary, the various parts are to a certain extent mutually exclusive and exist in opposition to each other.

2

Under the dictates of the economy

Ruling supreme over our present-day civilization is the economy. It is the driving force, end and means, all in one. It dictates the course of things. The utilization of natural resources, social values and the policies of the state are all in its powerful grip. An 'economization' of all spheres of life has taken place. Every one of our activities, from birth to burial, runs the risk of being marketed.

Since the beginning of the seventies, our modern and prosperous civilization has entered a serious crisis. Having thrived for decades, the industrial-social system is today shaking in its very foundations. Whether we want to accept it or not: we have pushed development, especially in the second part of the twentieth century, to its economic, social and ecological limits. The economic crisis, the growth crisis, the work crisis, the environmental crisis, the state crisis and the intellectual crisis which many people are going through, are more than temporary and passing fits of weakness. Rather, they indicate a deeper cause for alarm. We therefore have sufficient reason for pursuing this subject further, even if it seems to go beyond the scope of this book.

Initially our modern industrial society was fired by scientific and technical progress. It set in motion the industrialization of the economy, it brought about and spread methods of mass production and the worldwide exchange of goods – not to mention that of people. 'Prosperity for many through economic growth', is the catchphrase behind our high living standards. It was a recipe that worked very well for many years. It is said that about two-thirds of the total value of all products ever produced (the total world social product since the beginning of human existence) has been created in the short period of time between 1950 and 1980.[4] Believers in growth take as their (to them irrefutable) credo, the 'growth cycle' (see Figure 2): more production creates more work → more work creates more income → more income allows more consumption → more consumption requires more production → and so on. Or the other way round: more production calls for more consumption etc. One value is by necessity linked with the other. The one can always be justified by the other. Simple, logical and convincing. A cycle without end – this is what growth ideologists still believe and hope for, staring in fascination at the annual growth rates, spellbound at the figures for the so-called gross national product, the golden calf of prosperity statisticians. They deliberately overlook how false and deceitful this yardstick can be. An estimate based on the national product is a cost estimate and not a benefit estimate. The higher our total costs, the better off we shall allegedly be.

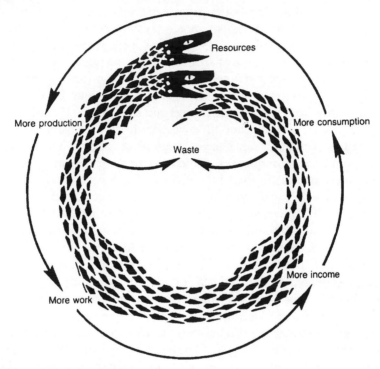

Figure 2   *The growth cycle.*

- The faster things break, wear out, go out of fashion, get thrown away,
- the greater the cost of disposing of the increasing quantities of waste,
- the more we spend to control air and water pollution and reduce noise,
- the more accidents we cause,

- the more chemicals we spray on our fields and the more drugs we take,
- the greater the number of patients in our hospitals,
- the more things we produce, even if we use them very little (a very good case in point is the over-supply of hotels and other tourist facilities, most of which are occupied for little more than two months in a year)[5] or even have to destroy because there are too many of them,
- the more . . . and so on and so forth . . .

. . . the more impressive is the gross national product and the more assured the claim of specialists in economic accounting that we are rich.[6] All this is presented as growing prosperity and progress, although the 'progress' figures are increasingly attributable to expenditure aimed at reducing the negative effects of economic growth.

'And now let's get down to work and increase our gross national product!' All those who fill their lungs and sing this song at the tops of their voices see nothing but the sweet fruit the explosive economic growth has brought us all. The very high price we have had to pay for it, the immense consequences, some of which are still latent and will manifest themselves to their full extent in a few years or decades and will have to be borne by coming generations, are of no consequence to these growth enthusiasts. Neither the irreparable damage to the environment nor the damage to the individual person or even bankrupt nations can shake them in their belief. They do not see the symptoms of the crisis, and, following the old-established method, they want to fight increasing unemployment with a further increase in production. We have thus reached the point where the official jargon no longer says that work creates production but that production creates work. We no longer work in order to produce – we produce in order to work.[7] In the name of job creation, Amen. Simple, stirring stuff. But the magic formula 'more production, more work' no longer functions. The latest technologies in the field of microelectronics, for instance, make it possible to reduce the human labour force and achieve even higher productivity. Also, it is more than probable that certain consumption limits have already been reached or will be reached in the near future. They certainly cannot be simply pushed further and further back at will. And yet, people cling to the 'magic circle' and declare they are acting in accordance with the forces of circumstance, which are growing stronger day by day.

The industrial social system, so successful for a long time, threatens to degenerate into a vicious circle. The once magic circle is turning into a snake with two heads. One head devours natural resources in the form of raw materials and energy, the other head has already begun gnawing away at its own tail. This serpent is now producing an ever-growing mountain of excrement, of non-renewable waste: matter and energy, which cannot be channelled back into the circle – which cannot be served up as fodder to head number one. Thus, it is lost forever and represents an encroachment and burden on the environment. It is argued that with the help of new conservation and protection technologies, the negative ecological effects could be reduced and the danger averted. But the argument goes on and says that in order to secure the necessary funds, further economic growth is needed more than ever before. Growth! So that we may pay for the costs of growth – and this not only where the environment is concerned!

3

The credo for a new harmony

This, then, is the scenario of our journey into the prosperity trap, of our gradual approach to the point where inertia is reached in the civilization machine. This situation suddenly strikes one as very reminiscent of one of Jean Tinguely's machine sculptures, for instance his mechanically-driven perforated bucket which ceaselessly dips into the well in front of the Stadttheater in Basel to draw water, only to lose it through its holes. But when the civilization machine starts generating nothing but inertia and when the means for maintenance and renewal have been exhausted, the parts of the machine wear out by themselves. The danger that then arises is that the wheels will turn more and more slowly until finally everything comes to a halt and falls apart. In any case, the perpetuation of current patterns of development holds little promise for the future as can also be seen from the conclusions of the report 'Global 2000', submitted in 1980 to the president of the United States. We shall quote it here as representative of many other world development models which have arrived at similar results:[8]

> If present trends continue, the world in 2000 will be more crowded, more polluted, less stable ecologically and more vulnerable to disruption than the world we live in now. Serious stresses involving population, resources and environment are clearly visible ahead. Despite greater material output, the world's people will be poorer in many ways than they are today.

Is a different outcome not possible? If it is possible, under what circumstances? Is there a turning point in sight? Must human welfare and the environment be sacrificed to the functioning of the economy? Must we 'produce' sick people in order to have a healthy economy?[9] Must we in the future, in order to get on, run twice as fast as before, as an economic expert recently put it? Shouldn't we instead take the foot off the accelerator if we want to win the race?[10] Should we not go one step back to view the thing from a distance and consider where the forces of circumstances are taking us?

Nobody could be so presumptuous as to claim that a better life model can be worked out immediately and laid on the table. Yet, doubts and questions about the accepted patterns can help. In addition, new knowledge, new proposals and experiments in all areas of science are necessary. While feeling our way forward in the sphere of leisure and travel, we intend to bear in mind all the characteristics of the social development we have just described and criticized. We want to consider how leisure and travel should be designed for a future that will be worth living.

What we consider as a desirable development for the future can be expressed in a few sentences on the basis of Figure 1. The principal long-term goal must be the restoration of harmony in the overall system. But harmony can exist only in a moderate 'not only . . . but also' situation, where society, economy, environment and state all complement one another; where the economy is again embedded in social relationships, and not the other way round, in other words, where the economy is again in the service of man and society; where the preservation of an unspoiled environment is a binding obligation and where every violation of this principle is punished like any other offence that destroys life; and furthermore, where the state must ensure the conditions without which a new harmony cannot come into being. All this can be achieved only if the trends shown in Figure 1 are channelled in a new direction and modified, so that we may come closer to a state of harmony. This means: a return to a more decentralized economy instead of a centralized one; more 'being' than 'having' in social and human values; greater awareness of the finiteness of natural resources instead of exploitation; more federalist instead of centralist state policies. However, the system will certainly not change direction and reorganize itself on its own. If something, or someone, has to make a move soon, then all of us must take an active part, build blockades, try to check the speed of development, and influence structures. And, most important, we must all be willing not only to think differently but to behave differently too.

Our image of a desirable future is, then, to find or regain a state of moderation and human measure, a 'harmonized, cooperative world, in which each part is a centre, living at the expense of nobody else, in partnership with nature and in solidarity with future generations'.[11] This description corresponds precisely to what we have in mind. Especially in view of our main subject, to which we shall now turn.

PART TWO

The holiday machine
or:
the recreation cycle

The shortest way to oneself leads around the world.

Hermann Graf-Keyserling

4

The motives of the mobile leisureman – travel between norm, promise and hope

Man in search of balance

The recreation cycle begins with man and his needs – with everyday people who become tourists and then return to their everyday existence. Indeed, these needs are the driving force of all human activity. Psychology teaches us that everybody is caught in numerous fields of tension formed by conflicting needs, for example:

Work – rest
Being awake – sleeping
Exertion – relaxation
Income – expenditure
Job – family
Freedom – dependence
Risk – security

To have one's life under control means to be able to find a balance between these needs. Like a tightrope walker, one must find a way between the extremes, which always means a 'both/and' rather than an 'either/or'. If the balancing act succeeds in all fields of tension, we are dealing with the ideal case of a well-balanced person: a trouble-free state without any tension that we may also call happiness.[1] If, however, one extreme predominates, it will cause feelings of dissatisfaction, deficiency or stress, followed by an urge to do something about it. The best way to achieve mental and physical balance between stimulation and repose seems to be a 'medium activity level'. No doubt, that level differs from person to person. There are people who need more quiet and rest and those who need more activity and excitement. In industrial everyday life it is very difficult to achieve, let alone maintain, such a balance over a long period of time. On the one hand, people are inundated with stimuli in the form of rush, noise and stress. On the other hand, many things are monotonous, unstimulating and one-sided: housing, the environment, the journey to work, work itself, even everyday leisure. Other key words are uneventfulness, sedentariness, lack of contact and mobility. Is it not strange that in colloquial usage the term 'everyday life' has, in fact, negative connotations? Everyday life is the sum of the negative aspects of existence. Dirt – noise – work – rush – school – trouble – pollution. All this is part of everyday life. Its descriptions abound with drab colours and adjectives expressing sadness: grey, monotonous, tiring, sad, boring. But – and this is the worst thing about it: doesn't our life consist of more workdays than Sundays and holidays?

The possibility of leaving, going on a trip, is obviously very important. Everyday life is bearable in the long run only if there is a chance to get away; otherwise people lose their balance and fall ill. Free time, and above all, travel are there to add some colour to this bare landscape. They are the vehicle for man's restoration – his re-creation; they heal body and soul and bring vitality and new meaning to life.

The social influence

At last it's the weekend, finally the holidays have arrived! Throughout the week or the year, people have counted the days, looked forward to this time, worked for it, made plans and preparations. There are so many needs they want to satisfy during that free time, so many things they had set aside to do later, important and even essential things.

One thing seems to be certain: these needs can be satisfied only by going away and not by staying at home, with the exception, perhaps, of a privileged minority; namely, the few people who have an enjoyable, creative, eventful job, who can determine their work load and their pace themselves, people who are free, who lack nothing, who live in a beautiful place where they can take a holiday on their balcony or in the garden. For them every day is a holiday in a manner of speaking. They do not need a vacation so badly wanted by everybody else, although they do not travel less for that reason. This privilege is enjoyed by only a few aristocrats of work: writers, painters, musicians, and professors for example, and some others who have managed to organize their lives conveniently. But all those who are stuck with work processes, life styles and residential situations typical of industrial society, obviously depend on 'comfort from the outside'. For them, relaxation and holidays are synonymous with travel, with getting away. Our society projects recreation and relaxation needs towards the outside. The polarization 'work and live here – relax there' is now generally taken for granted.

Cities have never been too concerned about the leisure and recreation needs of their inhabitants. Most towns are more or less 'work towns' and are unsuitable for relaxation and leisure. The process of urbanization with its negative consequences for the inhabitants still continues although for a long time all the signs have indicated that cities should be developed in such a way as to become more habitable. And yet, work places are still concentrated in city centres. Real estate prices are rising. Living space is shrinking. Cities sprawl out into the countryside. The network of roads linking the city with the countryside has been steadily growing. The few desperate efforts to save the old green area and a few places for recreation cannot change this: habituality and the quality of urban life are deteriorating even as we watch. The twofold division of man has been followed by a threefold one: work here – live there – relax somewhere else. Responsibility for satisfying recreation needs has not been accepted by city authorities. Rather, they have relied on the existence of the countryside, even to the extent of placing the onus of responsibility there, and thus avoided having to provide or pay for such amenities themselves. This has led to a worldwide division of labour between metropolises and their surrounding areas, although the roles have never been agreed upon and the costs (in this rather dubious partnership) are unevenly distributed.

The motivation of the individual person to travel, to look outside for what he cannot find inside, is produced not so much by an innate impulse – but develops primarily under the influence of the social environment, from which every individual draws his norms. The individual decision is socially predetermined, especially as regards travel and holidays. What our society offers routine-weary people is tourism, a variety of holidays outside the everyday world, extolling them as escape-aids, problem-solvers, suppliers of strength, energy, new lifeblood and happiness. The get-away offer should be accessible to everyone. After the 'right to holidays', the 'right to holiday travel' has now become a socio-political issue: tourism for all social classes. In fact, relaxation and holidays are now being identified with tourism; this suggests the need to travel, although both could be satisfied at home just as well if the necessary conditions were created. But this possibility is either being ignored or people have long since abandoned the fight for more habitable towns and more humane conditions. Thus, travel has become a social norm.[2] 'We are going away on holiday' is part of life in our civilization and has become rooted in our thinking as something taken for granted as normal behaviour. We don't ask: 'What are you doing during the holidays?', but 'Where are you going during the holidays?' While no particular reason is now required for going away for one's holiday, there must be a special reason for not doing so. In a society which is so preoccupied with travelling, we can find it hard to justify our staying at home without losing our social prestige. Prestige considerations and keeping up with the Jones's clearly play a role in deciding about travel, although not the most important one as some tourist theorists would have it. Like a second car or a second home, holiday travel is perhaps a so-called 'position marker', indicating a person's place on the social ladder. But since a trip round the world is now cheap for most people and a trip to the moon cannot be bought yet, the formula 'the further away and the more expensive the trip, the better', has long ceased to weigh with all classes of society. To spend the holidays near home or even at home, not to own a second car or a second home also brings social recognition today, even admiration, especially among intellectual or wealthy social groups. For those who have travelled most, have seen the world, who live in elegant homes and earn a great deal of money, it is easy to view mass travel with detachment. Be that as it may: considerations of prestige will probably always play some role in deciding about travel, though it is impossible to say how big a role – it should not be overestimated.

There are many other, less manifest, forces in our society which strengthen the urge to get away from home. For instance, the organization of the yearly working time and school holidays; the campaign and arguments of politicians in favour of a fourth or fifth vacation week; general information in the press, on radio and television, where holidays and travel are almost always mentioned in one breath; countless novels, plays and films set in holiday resorts and describing their atmosphere; general advertising and fashion, which breathe the air of the great wide world and which, in passing, also awaken the longing for sun, sand and sea, for unspoilt nature, for doing absolutely nothing or for wild adventure. The many songs ranging from Schubert's *Müllers Wanderlust* to *Viva l'España*, which sing about the pleasure of going away and being somewhere else; our dear friends, neighbours and colleagues at work, who tell us about their travel experiences as if they were the most exciting thing in the world; government-aided programmes aimed at promoting tourism; trade union sponsored holiday saving schemes; treatment in health resorts paid by health insurance; the granting of tax allowances for a second home abroad; travel as a prize for outstanding performance at work instead of bonus money; and so on and so forth.

When millions of people get on the move at weekends and during holidays, emptiness spreads over the everyday world. The leisure shock deadens and paralyzes the pulsing life of the city.[3] There are 'closed for the holidays' signs on shops; restaurants are either closed or serve only cold dishes. Who wants to stay in town then? People don't stay where nothing happens. Which means: let's go away too! And because so many people go away, nothing does happen at home. Isn't there a kind of social pressure to do what everybody else does? And what happens to those who must stay?

All these influencing forces have the same message for weary people: 'Your expectations are called tourism.' They even make them believe that their need has always, in fact, been a need for tourism.

The promises of the paradise sellers

The timber industry processes timber. The metal industry processes metal. The tourist industry processes tourists.[4]

The conditions for those who sell holidays and promote tourism couldn't be better: the social factors we have described have produced a general climate favouring travel. Whether it is travel we want to fill our spare time with is a question nobody even asks any more. The consequences of such travel for people and the environment seem to get even less consideration. Tourism suppliers need only come with their offers to whet the travel appetite and persuade the last hesitating few that holidays at X or a trip to Y will bring them the fulfilment of their dreams: tourism as a well-earned, harmless and carefree pleasure, the sunny side of the street.

An ever more gigantic entertainment and pleasure industry is taking hold of our needs for leisure and travel, obliterating everything else. It is the industry of tour operators, of air, railway, road and sea transport companies; catering and entertainment contractors, builders of second homes and caravans, manufacturers of camping and caravanning equipment, planning consultants, architects, cable car manufacturers, ski and clothing industries, souvenir shops, casinos and lunarparks, the automobile industry, banks, insurance companies, etc. An industry with its own laws, and its own newspapers; for example, there is a magazine with the high-sounding name *Amusement Industry. International Trade Review on Leisure Equipment Technology*[5]; with its own conventions, fairs and exhibitions, all of it organized on a national and international scale. Everybody wants more business, a larger share of the market. They will all move heaven and earth and use well-contrived methods to reach their goal. The countryside, the most beautiful landscapes and the most interesting cultures around the globe form the theatre of operations of this industry. Competition is keen, but demand is great. 'Tourism is business not charity', 'To hell with paradise!' is how promoters of tourism talk.

The commercialization of recreation needs and their transformation into travel of all kinds follows the established rules of marketing. The techniques are the same as in selling cars, vacuum cleaners, detergent or other consumer goods. But because they deal in desires and dreams, landscapes, people and cultures, travel sellers, one would presume, carry a much greater responsibility. However, they don't seem to be aware of it – or else they simply do not want to realize it. The 'producers' of the item called travel are not charitable institutions but commercial undertakings, a fact to which they admit quite openly. Why a journey is undertaken is of no consequence to them – what matters is that it is undertaken. Their primary interest is the short-term growth of their own business and not the long-term development of a well-balanced tourist trade. It would be naive to censure them for it, because they act in accordance with established principles of the free-market economy. But today we must try to see where the limits of this freedom lie.

Preachers can promise their congregation a paradise after death. The tourist industry offers a paradise on earth.[6] How 'scientific' the methods they employ in doing this are, can be seen from the following extracts from the recommendations given by a psychologist for a successful design of the title page in travel catalogues.[7] It is a startlingly honest and in the eyes of the 'uninitiated' reader certainly a revealing and disenchanting description:

> First and foremost, a 'holiday mood' or 'vacation atmosphere' has to be conveyed, i.e. the counter-image of everyday life, expressing on the one hand informality, abandonment, serenity, freedom, pleasure, and on the other hand peace, space, time standing still, relaxation, a certain 'romanticism', a return to nature, to our origins, or a special, extraordinary experience . . .
>   It must show something beautiful, characteristic of holidays, certainly not something one can have at home (e.g. in the local swimming pool) or something that is reminiscent of the workaday life of the country of destination (e.g. the everyday appearance of the local population) . . .

When depicting people from a different culture caution is needed; they should not appear too strange, that is, they should not deviate too much from our beauty ideal, because that could give rise to prejudice; subconscious reactions of fear may also play a role then . . .

Typical holiday symbols, e.g. the sun, a parasol, a beach basket and the like can certainly also be used to advantage. This however, should be studied by each tour operator individually.

Here are a few examples of what seasoned copy-writers can think of and what arguments are used in holiday advertising: 'Togo, the summer land for winter blues, where the franc still buys something'. 'A terrific idea for a present: Togo under the Christmas tree. Because the best presents are the unexpected ones. So why don't you surprise somebody who expects it least with a Togo ticket. A successful graduate, or your very efficient secretary or somebody who is dear to you.' Or: 'Kenya instead of the cold! If you'd rather buy suntan lotion than heating oil: go to Kenya with Touropa.' Or the Club Méditerranée slogan: For two weeks quite close to real life – 'Pour deux semaines tout près de la vraie vie' – 'For instance in the Gulf of Gabes. Head in the sun. Feet in the water. Bungalows under the palm trees. Sailing. Surfing. Snorkelling. Table tennis. Tennis. Ball games. Archery. Filling up. Switching off.' Or: 'In a taverna, in the shade of a tree, on a small balcony or strolling along the harbour promenade, the locals spend their time in delightful idleness. What is more logical than to do like these happy folk and spend wonderful, lazy holidays?' Or: 'A not-to-be-missed offer: chalets, to be erected shortly, on a lovely southern facing slope, on the best location in an idyllic village with a fantastic unspoilt view' – 'Save your tax money with a chalet in beautiful Switzerland' – 'Where grass grows today, your capital can grow tomorrow'.

Those who want to survive in the tough business of winning the tourists' favour must be able to sing high and low, because the competition in this promising market is becoming keener every day. The name of the game is not the winning of a prize for fair play, but big money. The end justifies the means.

This, then, is such stuff as dreams are made on. The verbal and pictorial clichés have been the same for decades: the deep blue ocean, the white sand, the sunset, palm trees, beautiful tanned holiday-makers, picturesque fishing and mountain villages, happy and laughing, colourfully dressed locals, turqouise-green swimming pools, eternal sunshine, eternal snow, untouched landscapes, virgin ski slopes, opulent self-service buffets, parents and children radiating health and happiness, adventurous trips, imposing sights, exciting nights, sex life, and so on. A serene Sunday world, a world of illusions, only a clipping, a montage usually worlds away from reality; a holiday atmosphere in superlatives, seen through rose-tinted glasses, presented in the way people would like it to be, a world they yearn for. Nobody will argue seriously that people do not see through the clichés. But it is obviously pleasant to be seduced by them, again and again.

What life is really like in the tourist country and the seamy side of the sunshine business is something that the normal tourist learns little or nothing about. True, due to criticism of tourist trade practices and pressure from consumer protection groups, travel catalogues have recently become a bit more honest. They occasionally point out the differences between the tourists' own country and the country they are going to visit. They sometimes include even a request for considerate behaviour. But this is probably the limit on how far the trade will go: the new wind has been duly taken into account and now the claim that 'We are progressive' can be made. But to put one's own business in jeopardy is certainly something that nobody in the industry is going to do. After all, they are tour operators and not a society for the preservation of local customs. And as long as the competition does not change course and adopt a more critical marketing approach, one just cannot do it either, however much one would like to. Clichés is what people want and clichés they will get. Travel destinations are interchangeable at will. They can be leafed through just as one leafs through the pages of travel catalogues.

The complex world of travel motives and expectations

When individual people are asked why they go on a journey, as is done in psychological tourism research in some countries every year with large-scale interview studies, it is not surprising to hear the reiteration of all the reasons that feature in advertising and which are repeated over and over again in all tourist brochures and catalogues. In this sense, the motives of the individual person are to a large extent 'ready made' or secondary. In technical terms: 'A subsequent rationalization of the unreflected, primary (social) motivation.'[8] Also, many of the quoted motives are nothing but empty boxes, which every individual may fill with quite different contents. Subjective wishes are thus condensed, simplified, registered and presented in the given answer formulas and statistics. Though this is probably the only way of measuring holiday-makers' motives, the reality is much more complex than appears from the results of various studies. There are always several motives that prompt a person to travel, and this is also the explanation for the overlaps in the following table.[9]

Question: *'What were the main reasons for your 1986 (main) holiday journey?'*

To switch off, relax.	66%
To get away from everyday life, have a change of scene.	59%
To recover strength.	49%
To experience nature.	47%
To have time for one another.	42%
To get sunshine, to escape from bad weather.	39%
To be with other people, to have company.	37%
To eat well.	36%
To have a lot of fun and entertainment, enjoy oneself, have a good time.	35%
To do as one pleases, to be free.	35%
To experience a great deal, to have a lot of change (diversity).	33%
To experience something entirely different, see new things.	33%
Cleaner air, clean water, to get out of the polluted environment.	32%
To get exercise, to engage in light sports and games activities.	30%
To experience other countries, to see the world.	30%
To rest a great deal, do nothing, little exertion.	29%
To be pampered, go on a spree, enjoy oneself.	26%
To make new friends.	23%
To do something for one's beauty, get a tan.	23%
To travel a great deal, to move around.	21%
To broaden one's horizons, do something for one's culture and education.	20%
To pursue one's own interests.	19%
To do something for one's health, prevent disease.	18%
To refresh memories.	18%
To see relatives and friends.	16%
To have time for introspection, thought.	15%
To engage actively in sport, to get fit.	12%
To go on exploration trips, to take a risk, to experience something out of the ordinary.	10%
To have time for one's hobbies.	7%

Since the same person could name several reasons, the total percentage is over 100.

Many things remain hidden in the subconsciousness and cannot be brought to light by simple questions.

So much for the reliability of the information obtained from studies of tourists' motives and behaviour. But despite these reservations, their results are very instructive because they show the general direction of motives and provide pointers for judging the weight of each of the reasons given for travelling.

We have used the results of German studies for several reasons. The travel motives and behaviour of the German population have been systematically studied for over twenty years. In no other country can such a comprehensive body of information be found. Furthermore, an international comparative study shows that the habits of travelling holiday-makers do not differ essentially from country to country.

Little has changed in this motivation structure since the first psychological research of tourism in the early sixties. The order of priorities has remained the same. However, since the early seventies there has been a marked shift towards active holidays. The wish to sleep, rest and do nothing is mentioned much less often, while categories such as 'Be with other people, talk to people', 'have fun, have a change, enjoy oneself, play' and 'engage in hobbies' become more important. The unchanged main motive of travel has, for many years now, been 'mental hygiene', recuperation in a world which is experienced as counter-everyday life. Going a step further, these motives, and the phenomenon of travel in general, can be interpreted in many ways, little of which, however, can be conclusively proved. The literature on tourism is full of different explanations and interpretations. The truth will probably not lie in one or the other of these theories, but in a mixture of various interpretations. Which does not make the thing any simpler.

Travel is recuperation and regeneration

This theory says: travel restores bodily and mental strength used up in everyday life, at work, school and in the family. It is a recharging of batteries; lubrication and oiling of the engine; minor maintenance on weekends, main servicing during the holidays. Taking a rest from everyday life in order that everything may run smoothly again and that productivity may remain high. The summer grazing of milked cows for future filling of the norm.

The number of sick is greater today than immediately after the Second World War. Our civilization has freed us from a large part of manual work, but in exchange we have had to buy such sedentary diseases as heart and circulation disorders. The so-called prosperity diseases have also become much more frequent: diabetes, high blood pressure, cancer of the respiratory tract as a result of cigarette smoking, alcoholism and many others. And what is especially striking: about half of the diseases are not of a primarily organic nature but the consequence of nervous stress, another product of the modern age.[10] Free time and holidays in order to fill up on health seem to be more necessary than ever before.

Travel is compensation and social integration

Travel compensates us for what we miss in everyday life. What people want is to find a compensation for the one-sided demands of their working life: they want to do and experience something that is different from the everyday routine, they seek diversion from the daily monotony, they long for fun and amusement. Increasing socialization, says this theory, drives people to take a holiday from society and escape into a world of leisure, which is relatively free from social and governmental constraints. After the trip they return willingly to the stable and familiar situation of everyday life. Tourism becomes a safety valve for letting off steam, a drug (as socially acceptable as aspirin) which temporarily kills the pain, but does nothing to cure the disease itself. It provides a way of channelling the disappointments over the impossibility of achieving one's aspirations into socially acceptable pursuits.

Travel is escape

This, most frequently quoted theory, says that the main motive for travelling is the wish to escape. It sees the modern industrial world as a prison from which its inmates want to break out. Working life being in fact ugly, the environment mostly unpleasant, monotonous and polluted, a compulsive and irrepressible urge to get out of it all emerges. According to this theory, tourism is assuming unmistakable characteristics of a mass flight from the reality of everyday life into an imaginary world of freedom. Because the everyday situation is unsatisfactory, people try to avoid it, at least temporarily, by travelling. What they want is to get away – though in a civilized manner – for a short while. It is the journey to the promised land. The flight to this imaginary outside world can also have the characteristics of escaping from oneself. The fear of inner emptiness and boredom, the thought that the holiday could be as lonely as solitary confinement or as boring as the assembly line, leads to an obsessive search for new experiences.[11] The tourist industry, says one of its most vociferous critics, offers only temporary respite, but in so doing, enables one to avoid the responsibility of changing one's situation to something from which it is no longer necessary to escape.[12] Having said that, we should add that such a flight is not necessarily away from the daily routine. It could be an answer to a back-to-nature call. To fresh air as opposed to our polluted city environment. Or it could be that people are fleeing from the climate: from rain to sunshine, from the cold to the heat. This is a motive which determines the great North-South migration of tourists and which always features prominently in tourist trade publicity: 'When our roads are covered by dirty slush, when the sky weighs as heavy as lead and it seems the sun will never shine again, wouldn't you rather be . . .'

Travel is communication

Establishing contact with people, in contrast to the anonymity and alienation of everyday life, is an important aim of holiday-makers. They want to spend more time with their family and close friends as well as make new friends and acquaintances. All this is much easier during the holidays, since the atmosphere is more casual than at home. But, as we are told by psychologists, the chance to find human warmth is not limited to the small circle of the clan.[13] The submersion into the big thundering holiday herd trotting through the leisure pastures can also produce the feeling of security. This mixing with like-minded people creates an archaic feeling of pleasure absent from everyday life with its tendency towards isolation and alienation at the work place, in high-rise blocks of flats or in the standardized suburban family-house colonies. Tourism, with its masses of people, is interpreted as a chance to establish contacts and to feel at ease among the many other holiday-makers in a kind of community: togetherness enhancing new experiences, tourists among themselves. The wish to establish some kind of contact with the local population is at the bottom of the list of motives − at least judging by the results of some studies. But other studies indicate that the number of tourists who would like to get to know the host country and its people better is much greater in reality than is generally assumed.[14] In many people, however, this apparent readiness is suppressed by uncertainty, inhibitions, lack of practice and experience. People don't quite know how to do it. So they don't. But even if this is the case, one thing is certain: the desire for contact with the native inhabitants in the country of destination is not a primary or urgent need for most tourists.

Travel broadens the mind
A look at the list of motives confirms that to: 'Broaden one's horizons, do something for one's culture and education', 'experience other countries, see the world, meet local people', or 'experience something entirely different, see new things', do *not* belong to the dominating group. Culture? Did you say culture? Other things are in the foreground. Cultural needs can be easily satisfied with homeopathic doses, that is, with the usual sightseeing tours. And yet, there probably are tourists who would be ready to experience something more or something different. (See above.)

Travel is freedom and self-determination
Freedom is, in the final analysis, the ability to make one's own decisions about a course of action. Travel liberates us from obligations. We can break loose from the 'must', from the order and regulations which oppress us in everyday life. We can finally do what we want and what we think is right. We can also do nothing. We are free, unrestrained, our own masters. For the German theologian and tourism researcher Paul Rieger, holidays are perhaps the only and last basically ungovernable and uncontrollable remnant of human freedom in our society. It is the most liberating form of leisure, because we can leave the habitual environment and, for a while at least, distance ourselves from it. Rieger believes that the various degenerations, massivity, clichés and primitivism do not change the fact that freedom *is* experienced during holiday travel.[15] Travel is double free time: it frees people from work *and* from home. Many, of course, do not know what to do with this unfamiliar and sudden liberty, or with themselves, because they lack the practice and the confidence and therefore in their need for help, turn to what is offered by the tourist industry. This does not make them 'manipulated puppets', far from it. It is, however, indisputable that the present pattern of tourism does not encourage the exercise of freedom and self-determination. Pattern F still dominates. To resist being pressed into it requires a great deal of initiative and independence.

Travel is self-realization
We have probably all experienced becoming aware of our own reality in places where everything is unfamiliar and strange. Travel, says this

theory, is a chance for self-discovery. Holidays provide an opportunity to confront the Self, to test one's soul, to come to terms with oneself, to measure oneself against others and discover one's own abilities. Beautiful as these chances offered by travel may sound, holiday-makers do not seem to be really aware of them, and as a motive for going away it is certainly at the bottom of their list – though it may be hidden, lurking behind other motives.

Travel is happiness

In literature and experts' discussions on travel and holidays the most common catch phrases are: 'the most memorable days of the year', 'a sparkling two weeks spent in a festive atmosphere', 'the happiest time of the year', 'happiness in its most accessible form'. In a recent study by the Starnberg Study Group for Tourism, human happiness is described as a harmonious state, trouble and tension-free, combined with a certain degree of self-realization. The probability of experiencing this state of happiness is supposed to be much greater during the holidays than in everyday life.[16] Holiday expectations consist of images of happiness – the journey away from routine as a kind of second life, the arteries of which have been pumped full of our wishes and hopes. Travel is more than a new form of stimulant in our consumer society. Those who travel want to find a joie de vivre. Not only a vacation, 'a temporary liberation from service', but a vacation, in German 'ferien', from the Latin 'feria', meaning 'festivity' and 'celebration'. This is what holidays should in fact be: the expression of sensuality, happiness and harmony. But isn't it hard enough to find even a little happiness, not to mention the other (fulfilled) Self, on a beach squeezed between endless lines of cars and towering blocks of houses. Be that as it may, the holiday-maker's subjective freedom remains one of the great chances for personal happiness even though in reality it is often squandered.

Travel is . . . The list of motives could be expanded at will. The contradictions would then be even more numerous. But it is these contradictions that reveal the true nature of tourism – a scintillating and multi-faceted part of human and social reality. Indeed, every tourist is probably motivated by more than one of the reasons we have outlined above, depending on his social status and form of travel opted for. We must not forget that the traveller himself is a mixture of many characteristics that cannot be simply assigned into this category or that one.

But are we to content ourselves with this diffuse picture of travel motives, in which everything or nothing is possible and which does not help us in our investigation? A closer analysis will reveal two things that run like a thread through all the studies: first, travel is motivated by 'going *away* from' rather than 'going towards' something or somebody. To shake off the everyday situation is much more important than the interest in visiting new places and people. This is closely connected with the second point: travellers' motives and behaviour are markedly self-oriented: 'Now *I* decide what is on and it should be good for *me*.' These two observations are very important for our further considerations. They reveal already at this stage the difficulties of a harmonious tourism.

The list of motives shows quite explicitly that even if motivation is not always negative, i.e. based on the wish to escape, the 'going away from' element is always the dominant one. Where the journey leads is not so important, the main thing is to get away from the routine, to switch off, change the scene. To this extent travel destinations are altogether interchangeable.

What matters is that there is snow for skiing, sunshine for getting a tan, the sea for swimming, opportunities for gregariousness and entertainment. The 'toward' element, the positive motivation of experiencing something, the readiness to learn something about other people, other countries and cultures and about oneself, all play a subordinate role. By contrast, the emphasis on the Self manifests itself almost everywhere: the tourist doesn't receive orders any more, he gives them. He wants to get the best of things, have fun, be pampered. Perhaps even play a role that would be impossible in everyday life. For a short while, he wants to appear as 'King Guest' and be treated as such. He wants to have the feeling he is somebody. It is a kind of self-realization, very possibly at the expense of others. People are either not aware of it or they think it is their right. Nevertheless, whatever the motives – the weekend in the country, the cultured educational traveller, the photo-amateur on safari, the sun worshipper on the beach, the adventurer in the jungle and the skier in the mountains – egoistic motives, whether we realize it or not, are always first and foremost. Furthermore: as long as such motives predominate, as long as the visited country and its people are taken only as a holiday setting, there is no hope for a 'better' tourism.

5

Behaviour and experiences while travelling

What do people do, what do they experience when they travel? How are their numerous wishes and expectations reflected in their behaviour? What are the most conspicuous characteristics? Do they follow a pattern?

The favourite holiday activities

A look at the list of holiday activities of German tourists shows how wide the range of tourist activities is. Active recreation is perhaps overvalued because it is more prestigious but the list contains no surprises. It shows all the usual things that are done on holiday. What transpires is both the clichéd pattern of the questions and probably also the holiday-makers' behaviour. To this extent holiday activities look quite harmless, but the point is that what the particular activities are is probably much less interesting than the way they are pursued.

An interesting and frequently discussed question is the apparent contradiction between tourist motives and actual tourist behaviour. The typical tourist alleges he wants peace, a change and something totally different from everyday life, yet he is found in crowds, in concrete holiday towns, in artificial tourist landscapes, in a Disneyland atmosphere, and in situations that are sometimes more complex, more restless and less free than the situation at home.

Question: *'Here is a list of activities that can be pursued during the holidays. Which of them would you choose for your (main) 1986 holiday?'*[17]

Go for walks.	70%
Go swimming.	66%
Go on trips, see the surroundings of the place.	65%

Talk to other people.	58%
Sunbathe.	56%
Go to restaurants, go out for a drink.	55%
Take photographs, make films.	52%
Go window-shopping, shopping.	52%
Sightsee, visit museums.	50%
Sleep, rest.	50%
Go on walking tours, hike.	46%
Write letters and postcards.	46%
Lie on the beach or by the pool.	44%
Try the local food.	42%
Read books, novels, comics, newspapers, magazines.	41%
Listen to the radio, watch television.	36%
Go dancing, go to the discotheques.	26%
Play ball or other games requiring physical exercise.	26%
Play party games, cards.	25%
Have parties, barbecues, make camp fires.	24%
Play with the children, do things.	22%
Engage in sport.	20%
Visit animal parks, national parks.	20%
Go to cultural events, lectures.	17%
Go to folk festivals, amusement parks.	12%
Solve riddles, crosswords, brain-teasers and the like.	11%
Go to Mass.	10%
Go to the sauna.	5%
Undergo a cure, take medicinal baths, massage.	4%
Engage in hobbies.	4%
Go to the cinema.	4%

Since the same person could name several activities, the total percentage is over 100.

Of armour, exceptions and clichés

There are several characteristics typical of tourist behaviour, looking at which may help us understand the conflicting and strange nature of tourism. The first observation (applicable to all of us) is that when we go away we don't really leave our everyday lives behind, but take them with us rather like a passenger on the pillion seat. We can never truly get them out of our systems however much we try. They always catch up with us. In any case, we do not suddenly become different persons when we travel, we are all shaped by our everyday style of living. We have many deep-rooted habits and needs, we behave in set ways and these cannot be simply shaken off. Whether we want it or not, we take them along on our trips. Into our suitcases goes a large portion of everyday life – all the many things we don't want to be without during the holiday. The car, itself a habitual item of comfort, is loaded with a great deal of domestic bric-a-brac. And when we do go, we don't do it in a leisurely way, taking our time as one would expect. Oh no, we go possibly even more hectically than usual. Impregnated with the work ethic, trained to be punctual and disciplined, and unfamiliar with the art of using free time in a sovereign way, holiday-makers promptly fall into the habitual trot. Thus the very start of the holiday often turns into a sort of race, a rally, in which the destination must be reached via the shortest and quickest route. It has been shown that about 60 per cent of all motorized holiday-makers race to their destination without a single stop; some people cover between 1000 and 2000 kilometres in one day.[18] Having arrived at the scene of their dreams, many tourists behave in much the same way as they do at home. It is as if they had simply moved their weekend-at-home several hundred miles away in order to enjoy it in a different setting.[19] We are told by psychologists that the feeling of experiencing something different from everyday situations is not brought about by unusual activities, but by the uninhibited pursuit of all the things we are used to doing at home.[20] Even when we do something different, we do it at our usual pace: we get up at a set time, we go to the beach, we eat, we sleep, always punctual and reliable. Indeed, the contrast to life at home must not become too big. We have our local newspaper sent to wherever we are spending the holiday, and deplore the inefficiency of the local post office if it is not on the breakfast table where it should lie every morning.

For many people the holiday experience exhausts itself in the feeling that they do not have to work and that they are not at home. They do not ask for much more. The rest can or even must be exactly the way it is every other day of the year. The holiday resort is just an exotic backdrop. If it is too strange, too different from the habitual scene, it produces a feeling of unease, even insecurity. People want the familiar. They're accustomed to certain things and amongst them they feel at ease. The same food, the same drinks, the same language, the same games, the same comfort as at home. 'You shouldn't change your habits when you visit foreign countries . . . instead enjoy the comforts of international standards . . .' says the advertisement of a hotel chain. 'We make you feel at home', is a perennial phrase of tourist brochures. Copywriters know exactly what to appeal to.

If all this is true – if the flight from everyday life leads us unfailingly back to it, the obvious question is why not stay at home? It seems that what accompanies us on our trip is a 'milieu-armour' – a kind of cloak which we cannot get rid of, but through which nobody from the outside can get to us either. Furthermore, we drag along all the evils of residential and industrial areas from which we would like to escape, and bring them as presents to our hosts: traffic problems, air pollution, noise, metropolitan architecture, alienation – to name but a few.

The self-oriented motivation produces another characteristic trait of tourist behaviour, which sometimes makes travelling an aggressive, reckless and colonialist phenomenon. 'Hello, here we come!' Away from home and free. Free at last of all constraints and considerations for others. Do as one pleases: dress, eat, spend money, celebrate and feast – the way we have wanted for so long. Have one's fling, let off steam. Regardless of what other people may think about it. After all, we have paid for it. Tourists often display peculiar behaviour in their new-found liberation, carrying on in a way that would be regarded as highly unusual and even bring censure and sanctions at home or at work. They feel and behave like some kind of exceptional people. They break the fetters of everyday rules. They are equally unwilling to observe the norms of the country they are visiting. Even elementary manners suddenly go by the board. Everything else is taken along, but manners are often left at home. The 'have-a-good-time' ideology and the 'tomorrow-we-shall-be-gone-again' attitude set the tone. Responsibility is rejected, egoism rules. And when entire groups of people behave in this way, the result is bewildering.

Another characteristic typical of tourists is their wish to find the confirmation of their image formed of the holiday area, of the dreams and pictures that are mainly shaped by tourist trade advertising. We all have them in our heads when we go on holiday and we want the promise to be fulfilled, even if the picture is more often than not a cliché reflecting only a part of reality or even distorting it outright. The tourist industry takes this wish up on the spot and offers a picture-postcard world. What is supplied both creates and satisfies the need to see as many familiar, safe and enjoyable things as possible surrounded by an aura of exoticism. This leads to the development of operetta-like tourist resorts which have nothing to do with reality and which are pure theatre, provided artificially with all the expected scenery.

'Foreign' elements are administered in small doses and in a palatable form and are reduced to the picturesque. The trip to the very photogenic, poor, but happy natives in Black Africa is a tourist cliché just as much as the encounter with the always yodelling, flag-waving, alphorn-blowing and cheese-carrying Swiss herdsman in his beautiful costume and his Sennenchäppi. But who cares about slums in a developing country or the assembly line in an industrialized country? After all, we are on holiday. Is it really conceivable that a meaningful contact with the foreign environment, with the host country and its people could take place under such circumstances?

Example 1:   Holidays in the ghetto

Peaceful hiking away from crowded roads, holidays down on the farm, an educational trip to places of historical and cultural interest, a cruise, a safari, holidays at a seaside resort, sailing holidays on a lake – there are many forms of tourism and it would take many books to describe them all. We shall therefore single out two examples calling them 'holidays in the ghetto' and 'alternative travel', because they may be taken, to a certain extent, as two extremes; all the other forms of travel lie somewhere in between and contain some elements of them both.

On the one side, then, holidays in the ghetto, holidays in artificially created reservations, made to measure for tourists. This category comprises the many new hotel complexes, holiday towns, parks and settlements, which have not been built as an extension of an existing village, but have been placed on the formerly green alpine slopes or on what was once a sand beach as a kind of test tube product. They are a familiar sight: the new ski resorts in the Alps, the little 'Manhattans above the clouds', the bed citadels, hotel palaces and holiday settlements all over the globe. They all look alike. The heavy 'Hilton style' predominates, and the scattered 'Tahiti style' has also become popular recently. Not only are most tourist centres interchangeable but they all have the necessary capacity to process the tourist flood when it comes. The most important part of the foreign environment is the beautiful location serving as scenery. That and some native personnel are all the local ingredients such tourist centres will include. They are completely self-sufficient and offer tourists everything their hearts may desire – so they do not need to go outside them. Tourists arrive there via the shortest possible route or are even flown in. After a few days or weeks, they leave the place of their dreams in an equally direct manner.

The most sophisticated version of ghetto tourism has certainly been developed by the Club Méditerranée which, although sneered at and derided by cultural critics, is immensely popular with its members, who return to it year after year. I believe that the Club and all those who imitate it offer a basically honest formula for a relaxing holiday. Indeed, this form of travel may have, in the final analysis, the least negative consequences for the host country and its population. The formula is honest because it incorporates many of the actual tourist motives and admits quite openly that its only aim is total recreation and relaxation for the Club members. No effort is spared round the clock to realize this aim. 'The idea behind Club Méditerranée is as old as the Fall of Man', says the Club in one of its own handouts.[21] 'It is the idea of a paradise, a Garden of Eden, in which people are free and unconstrained and everybody can be happy in his/her own way, regardless of whether it is in a sunshine village in the Antilles or in a snow village in the most beautiful part of the Alps.' The locality, or rather the surroundings of the Club village are not so important and can almost go unnoticed by tourists. The village is fenced off from the outside world by enclosures, turnpikes, gates and strict monitoring, so that the holiday-makers inside can pursue their leisure undisturbed. But doesn't the fence – and this certainly has its advantages – also protect the locals from the tourists? Inside, the club members can thus enjoy total freedom and abandon themselves to the consumption of the package of concentrated experiences. How lively things can be in such a club has been observed by Horst Hachmann in a German Aldiana Holiday club in Africa. Here is an amusing extract from his description of it:[22]

> By comparison, work in the office is restful. Here is how Karl-Arno from Klein-Flottbeck spent a Tuesday: at 8 o'clock he won the first match in the tennis tournament, at 9 o'clock the second. His sailing lesson had started in the meantime at the nautical club and Karl-Arno rushed to the beach making the soles of his Adidas shoes glow. For the next two hours he manoeuvred the catamaran around the turning buoys with such great skill that he earned the praise of the handsome sailing instructor. He had just enough time to gulp down a few mouthfuls of the enormous lunch buffet – he even went without the lobster and ice-cream, the onion soup and fillet steak – to make it in time for the volleyball team. At 4 p.m. he won, in passing, the freestyle swimming race in the Club Olympiad and just after was infuriated when he had to leave the Bingo empty handed. During that time he missed out on the date with Miss Adelinde from Wuppertal, with whom he had wanted to have a whisky-on-the-rocks at the pool bar. Adelinde found comfort with the goalie of the handball

team. At 6 p.m. he was so exhausted that he served three double faults in the semi-final of the tennis tournament and was eliminated. But he was again very much on the floor in the Club Lion contest – and as the clock struck 4 a.m. he had persuaded Miss Adelinde that it had only been his too busy schedule that had kept him from their rendezvous. Arm-in-arm, they walked to the next fixture. . . .

Those who do not want to participate in all of this need not. There is room for being alone and doing something on one's own, even within the Club. Here is what the theologian and holiday psychologist Paul Rieger asked himself after spending a holiday in a Club:[23]

'Where in fact did I spend my holidays? Was I in Greece? The answer is 'no', because Greece with its shores, mountains and stone-pines, with its villages, donkeys, sheep and village cafés remained far away outside. Was I on holiday then? Well, yes and no. Certainly, the sun, the sea, rest and a great deal of relaxation were there. But discovering oneself, experiencing the country and its people were far in the background. Where had I been? Simple. For two weeks I stayed in the world's biggest holiday theatre consisting of buffet luncheons, sport, fun, entertainment, glamour and glitter. The club idea is a grandiose effort at creating a sophisticated holiday environment and those who can go along with it will be happy there, returning home relaxed and full of pleasant memories. A holiday cannot be more than that.'

Paul Rieger is probably right. A vacation cannot be much more, not if we take into account the current state of affairs and certainly not if it is to be accessible to millions of people, possibly to everyone. Viewed in this light, the club formula and other big tourist centres, contemptuously called ghettos, have a great deal of honesty about them, not least because they offer exactly what many tourists want from their holidays . . . providing they are prepared to admit it. True, there are some questionable ingredients in their recipe – but this also depends on one's point of view. For example, the fact that the Club imports many items, ranging from food to personnel, must be felt as a slap in the face for the host country. Among these imports are many things that could very well be supplied by the local economy. The indigenous population feels it is being exploited because the economic benefit is small and they are often left only with the crumbs. This is the reason why in quite a few places the locals openly criticize and reject the Club. Equally inexplicable and unnecessary is the daily 'super-buffet' at the Club, which would provide a princely meal for three times as many people. Even many Club tourists, used to abundance and prosperity, feel ill at ease when they see what ends up in the refuse bin. And what do people in

Third World countries think when they watch such gourmandizing going on over the fence? Another point of criticism of the Club formula that I must mention is the way the ghetto opens briefly and tourists are taken on a lightning tour to see and photograph a few animals, temples and natives, so that they get some contact with where they are and have something to take home. The indigenous living conditions along their trail change rapidly and profoundly, especially in Third World countries. The tourist no longer sees the original foreign environment but rather a product he has helped to create: corrupt living conditions, pushy sellers, toadying and xenophobia. Equally damaging and humiliating can be the use of local culture in the form of meaningless folklore entertainment for the tourists in the ghetto. The most striking examples come again from developing countries: black girls performing dances of religious origin by the pool, gaped at by Cuba-Libre sipping tourists, discussing which of the girls has the most beautiful breasts and which of them would be the easiest lay.

Example 2:   Alternative travel

'There are many kinds of travel – from those designed for masses of tourists, to anonymous journeys following set patterns. And then there is travel for special people, people who like to do things differently . . .'[24] 'Our travels begin where other journeys end' . . . 'Different from different . . .' As the above quotes show, alternative tourism is not a well-defined notion, but the term is coming to be used increasingly for various modes of travel: educational trips, adventure holidays, hiking holidays or the solitary journeys undertaken by globe trotters. The term is most often used for travelling in, or to, the Third World, but sometimes it is applied to other countries. The guiding principle of alternative tourists is to put as much distance as possible between themselves and mass tourism. They try to avoid the beaten track, they want to go to places where nobody has set foot before them; they want to do things which will bring them a sense of adventure and help them to forget civilization for a while. Alternative tourists try to establish more contact with the local population, they try to do without the tourist infrastructure and they use the same accommodation and transport facilities as the natives. They also want to get more information before and during their holiday. They travel alone or in small groups. So far so good. But this type of tourism is also questionable, perhaps even more so than other forms of travel.

A very good illustration of what has happened in the past ten or twenty years almost all over the world can be seen in the following little story:[25]

> There is the tale about the dropout, tired of civilization, who finds a lovely distant Greek island, inhabited only by natives; he is hospitably received by the Greeks and spends a wonderful, cheap summer. He goes back to drizzly grey Central Europe, tells his friends about the sun, the wind and the sea, and the following summer a few friends turn up on the island, they have a wonderful time, pay some rent and speak German. They book rooms for the next summer, when they take some more friends along, the Greeks get together and rent rooms, offer meals that are tasty to the foreign palates, they purchase a slot machine. One of them gives up fishing and takes the tourists out in his boat, a woman converts her house into a pension, one man imports Coca-Cola and chewing gum from the mainland, another learns some German, a woman forbids the children to play on the beach, another woman begins to weave for visitors . . . The following summer, reservations for the Greek island can be made at home, it is in the catalogue, the fishing village has become a 'destination'.

In this way alternative tourists unwillingly become the vanguard of mass tourism from which they want to escape. Unwittingly they set new market mechanisms going, although many of them, especially the young are professed opponents of consumer ideology. But they themselves have become a market! The proliferation of alternative travel guidebooks, each of them offering the latest tips in 10,000 copy editions, is one aspect of this phenomenon; another is the expensive equipment, the special sleeping bag, the camera, the back pack and the like. And even the most fanatical 'off-the-road freaks' use, as a matter of course, many of the facilities produced by mass tourism which they despise so much: cheap flights, airports, the tourist information service, to mention but a few.

Alternative tourism has, then, also developed into big business. Market researchers estimate that in the Federal Republic of Germany alone around one million people are fed up with holidays spent lazing away between deck chair, swimming pool and hotel bar and want to go after quite different holiday experiences: physical exertion, nerve tingling excitement, team spirit and camaraderie.[26] The new hit is called adventure travel. Not only powerful cigarette firms, but quite a number of specialized operators have entered this particular market. Adventure travel advertising is being given more and more space in the catalogues of the big travel agencies. There's nothing you can't find

. . . away from the routine and the anonymity. The leisure industry offers not only fulfilment but produces, where necessary, the corresponding wishes and yearnings.

People go away because they no longer like it where they are. They go just to get away from the grey and sad routine offered by work and home . . .

. . . away from the monotony of the assembly line, from cold rationality and oppressive technology, from the unfeeling world of steel, glass and concrete, from poisoned air and grey skies.

The infrastructure for breaking away. Bridging the gap between town and country, between routine and counter-routine, between toil and freedom.

*Congested demands on life's pleasures. On the modern motorways,
auto-mobility is increasingly cancelling itself out. The psychology of
congestion as a new field of study!*

Resort areas as 'therapy zones' for the masses. Only just built and already overcrowded – holiday cranes are never out of work. Here the sun-sea therapy . . .

. . . and here the snow-ski therapy. Where more and more people go seeking leisure, they often find less and less of it.

The cure works! Holiday people go away in order to recharge their batteries, consume peace, climate, landscape and foreign cultures, and then they return to defy everyday life for a while longer. Tourism as a big regeneration machine.

there! Each year further, crazier, more original, just to stay in business:

'Hiking in the Arctic' (participants must carry their own packs part of the way), 'Elephant washing in India' (only for those under thirty-three years), 'Across the Sahara by jeep', 'On dog sleds in Greenland', 'The Philippino safari to the half-naked Karinga men and women and to the Ilongo nomads, for whom the bow and arrow are still the most important weapon and your trousers a wonder of the world', 'With head hunters and cannibals', 'Stone age in Ceylon', 'Across Australia on camel-back', 'With your sleeping bag along the Nile' or 'By helicopter to survival training in the Canadian wilderness', testing the 'very limits of physical and mental stamina', after which 'you cannot be shaken by everyday stress'. This kind of travel is by no means cheap. On the contrary, this is exclusive travel for exclusive people at exclusive prices. But there is no escaping from tourism, not even for alternative tourists. They remain, despite trekking here there and everywhere, citizens of industrial society engrained in familiar tourist habits. Here are a few extracts from a trekking catalogue – with malicious comments added.[27]

> Trekking means: on foot – with bearers, mules or horses for heavy loads – far away from modern civilization on mountain trails used only by natives; hiking, exploring, sometimes climbing mountains and crossing deserts. . . .'

Would you like a bearer or a mule?

> Meals are prepared on an open fire, usually by the participants themselves; in some countries, e.g. in Nepal, Ladak, Rayostan, Borneo and on the journey to Kilimanjaro, you will be spoilt by expert local cooks. . . .

Gourmandizing in the bush! Mouth-watering, isn't it?

> This kind of travel does involve some roughing it. You must be willing to do without luxury for a while, but what you get in exchange is camaraderie with like-minded people, perhaps even new friends. . . .

Exertion in carefully dosed portions, a little simple life and a great deal of group dynamics.

> Our trekking is not synonymous with cheap travel. After strenuous trekking in the jungle, we certainly appreciate the luxury of a first-class hotel. The purpose of our trekking is not mere exertion but the adventure this kind of travel involves. . . .

After the hot shower, a deodorized and civilized person again. What a pleasant feeling!

> You will often spend the night in a tent, on a farm, in an Indian hut, in the house of the village chief or merchant, in temples and monasteries or even in the open. . . .

Do the locals still enjoy it after the twentieth time? Who cares . . .

> Since our trekkings take you, as a rule, to culturally interesting countries, we always start with a cultural programme, except for instance in Alaska, where you immediately plunge into the wilderness. . . .

Civilized travel – on safari! Organized, saleable, sanitized adventure with full board, catalogue price and risk insurance. A unique hit. What nobody considers in all this is what benefit the local population derives from being 'discovered', observed and questioned in its most private life. The passing tourist caravan does not have the slightest idea of how deeply it can disturb the emotional, religious, cultural and ecologic balance of the host country and its people.

Similar objections apply to another form of alternative travel, the so-called 'integrated tourism'. In Senegal, for example, the experiment has been going on for ten years now. Many things are different in it: next to their village the natives have built huts for thirty tourists in the same style and from the same material as their own houses. The revenue from tourist visits goes to a common till and is used for the development of their own village. Eight camps have been built so far. The visitors, rather than see the country from the perspective of the hotel ghetto and the photo-safari, are given the opportunity to participate in village life, and to live for a while under the same conditions and at the same pace as the natives. This is supposed to lead to a real rapprochement. Jacqueline Hénard describes it as follows:[28]

> In this primeval night we play a bizarre social game. Three groups squat in a semi-circle. Thirty-six adults on woven mats and roughly hewn tree stumps. Twenty Frenchmen, four Italians and twelve Germans behave as if they had never sat at a table, as if they found it normal to eat by gas- and torch-light, as if it were natural to be served tomato salad on small hand-carved wooden boards. Four black figures serve rice and chicken in enamel bowls. They address us by our first names and we do likewise addressing them. Cautious adaptation in a decolonized developing country. We play at life in an African village.

The well-intentioned integration of tourists into the village community is impossible in reality and basically not even desirable. The cultural differences are too great and the time too short to bridge them. Tourists are left with an instructive view through a crack in a door opened for a moment. The locals are left with the money. They make money on tourists and therefore like them. Understanding among peoples cannot be organized.[29]

The much maligned tourist

The most exotic thing about tourism are tourists themselves! Our society has a distorted attitude to these strange beings called tourists. Although most of us travel – and not so infrequently – what other category of people are criticized, accused, laughed at or derided as much as tourists? They are called the new barbarians, the golden hordes, the new masters. They are compared to locust swarms appearing like a plague, laying waste and then going on. It made him quite ill to think how his fellow-countrymen carried on in Third World countries, said a German minister for development a few years back. The sigh can be heard rising all the way to heaven: 'Lord, they don't know what they are doing!' Caricaturists the world over have made tourists their favourite subject, and booklets with cartoons about tourism can be bought in every bookshop. Whatever the tourist does, he does it wrong:

The ridiculous tourist, immediately recognizable by his camera dangling before his belly, his funny leisure clothes, pale skin, fat or half-naked body.

The naive tourist, inexperienced in travelling, speaking no languages, who can't find his way around, asks stupid questions and can easily be led up the garden path.

The organized tourist, who is dependent on the group and the guide and, like a sheep, feels well only among other tourists.

The ugly tourist, who behaves as if the whole world belongs only to him and does all the things he is forbidden to do at home.

The uncultured tourist, who spends the holidays lazing on the beach, doesn't care a damn about the country and people he is visiting and watches TV, plays cards and eats sausages and fried eggs, like at home.

The rich tourist, who can afford anything he fancies and does spend lavishly, who puts his prosperity on show and enjoys being waited upon hand and foot.

The exploiting tourist, who spends his holiday at the cost of other peoples and cultures and takes advantage of the poverty of others.

The polluting tourist, who flattens everything in the way with his car, pollutes the air with exhaust fumes, tramples over meadows and fields, leaves dirty rivers, lakes and seas and ruins landscapes.

The alternative tourist, who differs from other tourists, explores the last untouched corners of the earth, thus paving the way for mass tourism.

And, needless to say, a tourist is always the other person! Educated people, people who can speak foreign languages, and who have higher incomes and more experience in travelling, can camouflage their tourist role. They feel they are individualists and believe they are superior to other people – although basically their behaviour when travelling is the same. 'That's something for tourists', they say, and naturally exclude themselves, pleased that they have been able to see through it. For them, the word 'tourist' is an insult.

All this indicates that our thinking about tourism and tourists is still very much confused, otherwise there wouldn't be so much criticism around. But, the widespread reviling of tourists is unconsidered and unproductive. Are tourists really the infantile fools or reckless ravagers they are made out to be? Should we really blame the tourist for the fact that there is something unnatural and artificial about their role? Do they really carry the main responsibility for all the negative effects of mass mobility and worldwide tourism? Aren't they rather the culprits and the victims all in one: defenceless pawns that anyone can use and attack? Those who censure tourism are in fact not criticizing individual travellers, but the massivity of the phenomenon. The main problem of modern tourism is that of its huge number.

All holiday-makers feel like individuals even when carried along by the massive wave of other tourists, because now they themselves choose and decide their actions – including that of whether to go on holiday or not. The sum of many individual actions, however, leads to a mass cliché. Millions of people display similar behaviour. It is here the criticism begins. What is particularly disturbing about the phenomenon is that the problem of large numbers can be solved in part only by industrial methods, i.e. with standardization, mass production and high-capacity facilities.

The much maligned tourist is a person looking, quite legitimately, for his/her happiness, badly needing the subjective freedom supplied by travelling even if – at least in the eyes of the critics – it is perhaps not used very intelligently. The tourist is his own advocate and not an international ambassador; he is not there to aid development or protect the environment. It goes without saying, then, that he behaves in an egoistic way. Nobody has ever explained to him the consequences of his actions and drawn his attention to the responsibility that is his. The damage tourism causes to the people, economy and environment of the host area, especially in the long-term, remains hidden from the tourist. He has been left out of all discussion on the subject, even though he is one of the main protagonists. Tourists seem to enjoy some kind of special status and are almost more immune than diplomats. They are therefore carefree and ignorant rather than devious. To lay all blame at their door would be as wrong as denying their responsibility. But they should certainly be made aware of the situation!

6

The host population – what they expect and what they get from tourism

In the cycle presented in Chapter 1 of our book, the native population of the holiday areas are the people on the other side of the fence, the hosts, willing or otherwise. How do they view tourism? What are their motives, interests and needs? And what do they actually get out of tourism?

The silent local

'Tourists are the most dangerous of enemies because one needs them. There are various reasons why one cannot simply kill them as one did with enemies in earlier times. But one can be silent.' (From a Greek text on tourism in Crete.)[30]

Here one would expect the locals to be given a hearing. It ought to be possible to find studies in which they present their views, describe their own situation and their wishes, what they expect from tourism and under what conditions they will accept it. After all, it is no longer like in the old times when hospitality was a matter of honourable obligation and when one had to receive one's worst enemy as one's best friend. With the emergence of tourism, the admirable virtue of hospitality has turned into a trade and a source of profit. But in the big travel business it is obviously the needs of tourists and their promoters that count. What local people feel, think and want is less important. How else can one explain the fact that there is very little information about what they think of it all. For example, on the shelves of the library of the Research Institute for Leisure and Tourism of Berne University there are 5000 books about leisure time and travel and packed away in boxes are thousands of manuscripts, papers and newspaper articles on the same subject. However, even a perfunctory glance at this comprehensive documentation will reveal that most of it focuses on the tourist or on the interests of the industry itself. The psychology and sociology of tourism have so far been concerned only with the tourist's views and behaviour. Tourists are the market and the relevant studies are merely market research, commissioned and financed by the travel industry. Such research leaves us in no doubt about why people travel: the overwhelming majority of tourists go to a particular place not because of its people but because of the physical features of the country. The beautiful landscape and the climate are the main attractions. The fact that there are people living there is almost irrelevant. Why then pay any attention to them?

But the host population must take part of the blame for this neglect, for up to the present they have hardly made their presence felt on the market scene. Which is only natural when one comes to think of it, for the prime target of tourism is the countryside – rural areas, where the standard of living and education is lower than in towns. Thus, at the beginning of tourist development, the local population does and accepts everything that is demanded from outside, from tourist trade promoters and from their own government and entrepreneurs. They believe the promises: when they are told that tourism is their big chance, that it is of vital importance for the region, or, indeed, for the whole country. Nobody mentions the negative aspects. Once tourism has taken hold of the area and the locals realize what they have let themselves in for, disillusionment and more realistic attitudes replace the initial euphoria. But then it can be too late, because they have lost control over their own destiny.

It could thus happen – and still does – that tourist development takes place over the heads of the local population. Very few locals ever participate in it as equal partners, the few exceptions being smart business people and the upper classes. The locals are given to understand that they have to conform to the market, i.e. the requirements of the tourist trade and tourists if they want to get on the bandwagon. All this, of course, is in perfect agreement with a basic principle of marketing: produce what sells. It is the locals then, who must adapt to tourists and not the other way around. Nobody asks them whether this clashes with their own values and ideas and this is probably the reason why so little is known about the subject.

More recent research has attempted to study the effects of travel on the economy, the environment and the population of the host areas. For instance we are in the middle of a fierce debate about the impact of tourism on the local society and culture in Third World countries. But even there the main spokesmen are not representatives of these countries but worried intellectuals from the developed world. The voice of the host population is hardly heard at all. Even in highly developed, traditional tourist areas, local attitudes are seldom expressed unequivocally. The population of the holiday resorts in the Swiss mountains, for example, have learned to live with tourism and tourists and although they meet all or almost all of their guests' wishes, they are also glad when the season is over. They need the intervening time between each invasion of holiday-makers to recuperate from the last lot. They can then resume contact with neighbours and friends and become once again part of the village community. This was shown very clearly in one of the few studies dealing with the attitudes of the local population in a holiday resort in the Swiss mountains.[31]

But the pre- and after-season may soon disappear and with them the chance for the locals to get a break, for one of the aims of the tourist industry is to have an all-year-round season. Just how it is trying to boost the present slack out-of-season business is illustrated by an advertisement for the Spanish Ministry of Tourism published in Switzerland: 'I don't want to be one of the million tourists in Spain. But: some time in the spring or autumn, when everyone else except the Spanish has gone home, I'd love to go there.' That Spaniards like being alone from time to time and that such publicity may rob them of the chance, is not one of the considerations of this kind of advertising.

Economic interest dominates

The search for information about host population attitudes to tourism is hampered by another difficulty. Opinions about and expectation from tourism can be very different depending on which population or occupational groups are considered:

The first category includes people who are in continuous and direct contact with tourists: the personnel in the catering trade, in transport, in shops, travel agencies, etc. Because they depend on tourism and would perhaps be unemployed without it, they welcome visitors. Their attitude is not determined by 'inborn hospitality' or the 'joy of being of service', as is often claimed, but rather by a simple desire to earn money.

The second group of locals are the proprietors of tourist businesses – unless owned by outsiders – and some local industries which have no regular contact with tourists, for instance the building industry. For them, even more than for the first group, tourism is a purely commercial matter. It should bring as high a turnover and profit as possible; the manner in which this happens is of little consequence; the end justifying the means.

The third category consists of those population groups who are in direct and frequent contact with tourists but who derive only a part of their income from tourism. They live in or near tourist centres and engage in various activities, mostly farming. This group also includes people who live along the main travel routes. Their link with tourism is more remote in some ways and their attitudes often much more critical. Members of this group do see the advantages resulting from tourism, for instance extra income for farmers, but they also feel more critical about it and point out its disadvantages – such as interference with their private lives and environmental damage.

The fourth category comprises the large group of locals who have no contact with tourists or see them only in passing. Here a variety of attitudes is possible: approval, rejection, interest or indifference, the latter being the most common. Politicians call it a 'lack of tourism consciousness'.

Politicians and political lobbyists represent the fifth group. They would like to raise their fellow countrymen's living standards – and not least their own. There are hardly any politicians who do not either openly advocate or quietly support tourism – both for economic reasons.

Foreign exchange has always been the main argument for the development of tourism in Third World countries. True, no estimates have been made of just how much of the tourist money remains in the country after the various expenses have been subtracted: the money paid for imported food and beverages, for foreign-made devices and equipment for hotels, the wages of foreign personnel and the profit flowing into the pockets of foreign operators and owners. Something is left in the country's own coffers, but frequently not very much. Ironically, the most meagre profit is made in those countries which are in the greatest need of foreign exchange, for being the least developed, they must import the most in order to satisfy international tourist standards. In the most extreme cases as much as 80 to 90 per cent of the foreign exchange earned flows out of the country again before it has had time to do any good.

In addition to the foreign exchange argument, the most frequently touted benefit of tourism is its effect on employment and incomes. As a highly labour-intensive service industry, it is claimed to create many jobs. In Switzerland one hotel bed is estimated to create about 0.5 jobs in the catering trade itself and, indirectly, in a number of related industries. The figure for developing countries is three and more jobs per bed.

The tourist dollar does not stay long in the hotelier's wallet, however. Part of it – a large part – is spent on the purchase of goods and services. In this way, income is created for the butcher, the grocer, the supplier of furniture and many others. These incomes are spent in their turn to pay for the raw materials, etc. As long as the tourist dollar is not saved and is reinvested in the country rather than being spent on imports, it creates new income. This so-called 'income-multiplier' lies somewhere between one and four, depending on which country is being considered: it is higher in developed regions and lower in developing countries.

Nobody will dispute the fact that tourism has a considerable impact on employment and incomes: at least ten million people work in tourism the world over and many more millions live off tourism indirectly. But there is a reverse side to the coin, seldom mentioned in political discussions: jobs in tourism are mostly unattractive. Working conditions are hard: the hours are irregular, there is a seasonal overload, overtime is more or less compulsory and one is at the mercy of the guest. Earnings, on the other hand, are below the average. The range of professional and training possibilities is limited. Many jobs are unskilled and considered as socially inferior, for example the work behind the scenes such as in the kitchen or cleaning. Tourism-related occupations therefore enjoy very little prestige, especially in developed countries. Not everybody likes to serve others, to belong to the 'servant minority', to be a second class citizen. All these reasons explain the paradox in Swiss tourist regions, for instance, where young people continue to migrate to towns in search of better jobs and where there is a personnel shortage in tourism at a time of increasing unemployment.

Tourism has yet another political dimension: it should help bridge the economic gap between industrialized urban areas and agricultural rural ones. As such it is often regarded as the economic panacea for many so-called fringe areas, the only means of slowing down the exodus from the countryside, of improving the living conditions of the population in areas where agriculture cannot provide sufficient livelihood, or in areas considered unsuitable for industrial development and where there is nothing to sell except the sun, sea or snow. This natural wealth must be 'capitalized'. One also hears politicians declare from time to time that only tourism can end the rural population's isolation, help it to join in the general progress and participate in the blessings of prosperity.

This, then, is what host areas expect to gain from tourism, if, that is, any clear notions exist and are expressed in the first place. Economic expectations come first and foremost. 'We don't need tourists, we need tourism.' The statement, which comes from a tourist trade politician from Sri Lanka, is the most honest, concise and fitting description of the interests of host areas all over the world. In other words: we can do very well without the tourists, who poke their noses into everything and disturb our lives, but we need their money.[32]

The other effects – social, cultural and ecological, the changed life style, the loss of cultural identity and the impact on the environment – must be accepted as long as the money flows in. Tourism is not a charitable institution for the host area, it is business, for which one is prepared, explicitly or implicitly, to make quite a few sacrifices. It is, however, dubious whether the local population gets a square deal, whether it is not the others who get the lion's share in the business and whether the price that has to be paid is not much too high. But is there nothing else, apart from tourism, that can save the domestic economy from ruin? This question is being asked more and more often in many tourist areas of the world.

The unequal exchange and the unpaid social costs

'The locals supply the mountains and the good air, we lowlanders supply the capital.'[33] These are the words of the managing director from Basel of a cable car firm operating somewhere in the Swiss Alps. A correct business arrangement between equal partners for the purpose of the joint pursuit of common economic interests? The reality is different. The 'division of labour' between town and country, between province and metropolis is unequal and one-sided. One does not have to be a Marxist or an economist to realize that the motto of the deal is 'The guy who pays gives the orders!' This German folk saying succinctly expresses the state of play: the one with the capital has the biggest lever. In the tourist business the money comes from the city, from the rich industrial areas and metropolises – and it flows back there. The population in the rural areas owns the other two means of production required, namely land and work, yet these are sold all too

cheaply to the entrepreneurs from the city. In order to get a share in
the tourist business, the locals sell their land and labour at bargain
prices. Since many areas are eager to develop tourism, the competition is keen, so that, unless the region is already a popular and
sought-after tourist destination, it must accept any price offered by
the bidder. It is the merciless and ubiquitous law of supply and
demand. Big investors, large concerns or tour operators can
negotiate even more favourable terms, because the host areas expect
a particularly high benefit from their engagement. In poor developing countries, the profit for the industrialist is even higher, because
prices are particularly cheap owing to the low standard of living. It
should also be noted that the natural ingredients of the landscape,
namely the good air, the sun, the snow, the mountains, the hills, the
lakes, the seas and the beaches, are free commodities. They sit there
for general and unlimited use. They have no price and are, so to
speak, delivered free of charge.

It thus happens that many tourist areas sell their resources for a
song, without noticing that the transactions make them increasingly
dependent. Instead of the milk, they sell the cow. Examples of this
are legion. First, the locals sell off their land for building at low
prices to non-residents and thus give away the trump card in the
poker game about the control of economic development. The money
they get is barely sufficient to cover basic needs. And when land
prices finally rise, the locals are again left out in the cold, because it
is again the others who make a profit. Ultimately, the locals can no
longer afford to live, let alone build a house in their own district
because of the high land prices and rents paid by non-residents. This
kind of situation can be observed in various tourist districts in the
Swiss mountain areas.

A true business partnership can be said to exist only if the costs and
benefits are equally divided between the two parties. This is by no
means the case in the tourist industry because the many social costs
caused by tourist development are not borne by their perpetrators, i.e.
the various businesses and the tourists, but by the local population
alone. These costs do not feature on any bill and yet they can become
an intolerable burden for the local community.

In an opinion poll carried out in a holiday resort in the Swiss
mountains the locals were asked what the development of tourism had
brought them over the past twenty years.[34] About half the people felt
the changes had been positive, the other half thought they had been
rather negative. A very high first place among the positive changes was

given to general prosperity. Among the negative aspects the following were particularly emphasized:

People only think of money now.	79%
The sense of community has been lost.	53%
There are too many strangers.	46%
The appearance of the village has been spoilt.	45%
Family life has suffered.	44%
The landscape has been ruined.	43%
Only a few have benefited from tourism.	26%

Since the same person could name several aspects, the total percentage is over 100.

This, then, is the price that the local population in this district feels it has had to pay for economic progress. It is the social costs which do not appear on any balance sheet.

• How can one put a figure to the deteriorating quality of the environment that inevitably results from tourism, the change in the village and landscape, architectural, water and air pollution, noise, the upsetting of the balance of nature, the effects on animals and plants, the loss of natural beauty?

• How can one put a figure to the increased susceptibility to crises of the local economy, which sets in when rapidly growing tourism displaces agriculture and sucks in all the other economic activities, resulting in a precarious 'single-crop' economy, which depends entirely on the economic and political situation in the tourists' area or country of origin? What would happen should tourists fail to come?

• How can one put a figure to the profound change that tourism may cause in the society of the host country? The desire to imitate consumer habits and behaviour of tourists, the unease and dissatisfaction about one's own lot or even resignation because the living standards of tourists are so much higher, inferiority complexes, servility, the 'urbanization' or 'westernization' of the lifestyle, increasing prostitution, child begging and delinquency in many tourist areas in Third World countries, the temptations brought by the tourists' money and wealth?

• How can one put a figure to the effect on local customs, traditions and norms, the disrupted family and social life, the corruption of language, cultural standardization and adaptation to foreign taste, folklorism, cultural prostitution?

- How can one put a figure to the psychological stress suffered by many locals because they feel powerless in an order of things, determined largely by outsiders?

Some of these social costs weigh particularly heavily where there is a big development gap between tourists and locals, i.e. in Third World countries. But they can be observed, in varying degrees, everywhere where there is tourism. Attempts are often made to hide or embellish them, or present them as the unavoidable reverse side of the tourist coin. 'If you want to enjoy the advantages you just also put up with the disadvantages' is the argument. But this rule obviously does not apply to people from the metropolises. They enjoy all the advantages, while paying a relatively low price for them, and avoid the disadvantages. Nobody has ever considered the possibility of conditions being imposed on tourists so that the cost-benefit ratio would become more favourable for their 'hosts'.

Decision making by others – a high price

Since time immemorial all people and societies have felt one compelling need: be autonomous. Wars and revolutions have been waged to shake off the foreign yoke, to achieve freedom and regain the right to self-determination. Freedom and autonomy are man's highest values. Indeed, these demands are so fundamental and natural that they are not always explicitly mentioned and emphasized. But it should be very necessary to do so in discussions about tourism and its consequences. For whichever part of the world we look at, be it the European Alps or a developing country in Black Africa, the pattern is the same: the development of tourism has robbed the local population of autonomous decision making. We shall continue with the example of the Alps to illustrate how these processes take place.[35]

The Alps are one of the world's largest holiday areas: during the main tourist season about five million holiday-makers from various parts of the world join the local population of about seven million. In typical holiday resorts, tourists outnumber locals sometimes by twenty to one. Surrounded by large towns and agglomerations, the Alps are a model example of problems created by tourist development. The most sharply felt among them is, without any doubt, the gradual loss of independence in decision making. For the local population the Alps provide their home and their livelihood. They are also an area of extraordinarily beautiful and vulnerable natural resources. These dimensions are, however, increasingly pushed into the background by a third: the Alps have become a complementary area for a population from other regions. For the big agglomerations rural areas are merely suppliers of labour, raw materials, drinking water and energy, all of which are necessary for further urban growth, but above all, they supply recreational space. Over the years the processes of decision making have shifted from the Alpine areas to the centres of political and economic power. Decisions on investment in new tourist centres, including funiculars, motorways, power plants, industrial plants, water supply, second homes, etc., are made in Zürich, Geneva, Paris, Milan, Munich or Frankfurt. Business interests, in other words, override concern about the living conditions of the Alpine population or the preservation of the ecological balance and natural resources, although a deterioration of the environmental quality of the mountain regions also destroys their recreational value for holiday-makers – hence the phrase 'tourism destroys tourism'. These detrimental processes have been allowed to continue almost unchecked throughout the Alpine area, despite repeated warnings from various quarters and despite the devastating effects that strike the eye everywhere. Doesn't this best reflect the fact that decisions about the development of these regions are made outside them? Isn't it an indication that the local population is being swept aside by rapid development and that it is losing its ability for self-control? People from the town come with their own yardsticks. Feeling superior, since they have the money and most often also a better education, they usurp the area for business and recreation. For them, the landscape and the people are just consumer goods. When they have done, when they have seen enough or no longer like it, they go elsewhere. They are accountable to no one nor, for that matter, do they feel any responsibility.

Just how business promoters go about their business has been described step by step by Pierre Lainé.[36]

Step one
The Grande Compagnie – a fictitious company name – secures control over the land. Its arguments are irresistible: many jobs and a great deal of income for the local population, who could never set development going on their own. Finally, the Grande Compagnie succeeds in buying up the land at rock bottom prices.

Step two
The Grande Compagnie persuades the local authorities into participating in the investment and financing of the infrastructure – roads, water

supply, etc. – or, failing that, into placing these facilities at the company's disposal under very favourable terms. The company, in turn, accepts responsibility for getting everything into good running order and filling the hotels with guests. There are many cases where promoters take over completely, the local community ending up as a passive bystander. A case in point are the well-known examples of hotels financed from public funds, in which promoters have taken over the management, and by such means as 'profit sharing' and 'deficit guarantee' clauses have earned themselves an even bigger share of the cake.

Step three
The Grande Compagnie employs its own architects, building contractors, furniture suppliers, etc., in designing, building and furnishing the project. The reason given is that the capacity of the local trade is insufficient or that the work of the locals could not satisfy the taste of the international clientele.

Step four
The Grande Compagnie launches its product with hard marketing. The package price is paid in the city, before the holiday, and most of it flows back into the promoter's pocket.

Step five
The management of the installations is also handed over to the Grande Compagnie; on the grounds that there is no trained local personnel, the jobs go to outsiders.

Step six
Even most of the food and drink is brought in from outside – because of the international clientele.

It is in this or a similar manner that many new tourist resorts have been developed. But it would be wrong to lay all the blame on bad, greedy and power-hungry promoters. The image of the innocent, fooled and exploited local does not always apply. In many tourist destinations, the locals have taken an active part in digging their own graves. The biggest land speculators sometimes come from the local ranks and even hold the highest political posts. Some locals do, unquestionably, make a nice profit out of tourism, but they are usually a very small minority belonging to the propertied classes. It goes without saying that they are staunch advocates of a further development of tourism. But the majority of the local population has to put up with the disadvantages brought on by the loss of control over their own communities. Not only have locals been relegated to the humbler positions of service personnel and are no longer masters in their own house, they must also foot the bill for the social costs arising in the wake of tourist development. But local authorities in tourist areas are also responsible for misguided development. In their blind faith in tourism as a panacea, they have introduced a whole battery of measures aimed at attracting outside capital: tax relief and tariff reductions, subsidies, investment incentives, reduced building land prices, deficit guarantees, construction of infrastructural facilities without the obligation of repayment etc. In Third World countries tourism is among the most heavily subsidized branches of the economy. This is clearly a case of the most disadvantaged population groups subsidizing the holidays of the privileged members of the European and North American populations.[37]

Why has the loss of local autonomy – certainly the most negative long-term effect of tourism – been practically ignored? Why does the local population tolerate it? We have mentioned a number of reasons, but the determining factor is perhaps the very nature of the process: it creeps in, moving on soft soles and one only becomes fully aware of it when it has reached an advanced stage. Tourism is a kind of friendly conquest, which takes place not only with the acquiescence of the conquered, but at their explicit invitation. What people forget is that decisions made by outsiders are not only about capital. Tourism is like fog; it penetrates everywhere. Its particularity is that tourists arrive in person with their behaviour and their influence. They demand things which are unavailable here and have to be imported. And they don't stay in one place – they are to be found everywhere. As a result, new 'developments' mushroom. More money is needed to finance the growing infrastructural facilities needed for tourists. But in order to pay one must make more money – and more money can be made only if more tourists can be attracted. Thus more and more firms come to the area, more and more tourists come, etc. Soon the host population is in the minority; local labour is no longer sufficient – reinforcements must be brought in from outside. The number of newcomers and seasonal personnel constantly increases. Some tourists and business people stay on because they like it or because they see they can do business in the area. They move their home and office there. Being competent and well-educated, they hold the good professional posts. They are interested in everything, including politics, they are good speakers and have experience. They don't have to wait long to be given political mandates and then they wheel and deal on the highest level. The reins have slipped from the hands of the locals – slowly, almost imperceptibly. Foreign infiltration is total: from the outside by tourists and from the inside by the newcomers and immigrant labour force. This classical pattern is everywhere more or less the same. Whether we like it or not: modern tourism has colonialist characteristics – everywhere and without exception.

As has already been pointed out, these problems are almost never discussed. They simply happen and are tolerated as if they were natural and immutable developments. But shouldn't they be questioned if a 'better' tourism is what we are looking for? Aren't they the main reason for the much criticized negative consequences of tourism in the destination areas? Unless some fundamental changes are made in this respect, tourism will never rid itself of its worst elements; it will remain a special form of subversion, because it develops by infiltration and prospers on imported values and behaviour. It is a new and devious form of colonialism, because it creates, in a butter-wouldn't-melt-in-its-mouth way, a new dependence and exploits people and resources.

7

The encounter between tourists and locals

To communicate with you tourist is another
thing; when you all come to our Island, you tend
to keep to yourself and not trying to communicate with us. Communicate may be a big word,
but it just few word needed to be said to get
friends, and friendship is what most people are
looking for, to have friends you must communicate with other people.
*From a school essay by 14-year-old
Erwin Harris, Antigua, the Caribbean*

A meeting worthy of the name should be characterized by human
interest and not primarily a financial one, by a mutual wish to
understand and accept each other, by mutual esteem and consideration. In its present form, tourism cannot encourage the development of
such virtues on either side. The barriers are enormous and can hardly
be overcome. Most of them have already been described here, so we
shall not repeat them – it will suffice to point out some specific
characteristics.

Understanding among peoples?

In the early 1960s a leading tourism researcher wrote:[38] 'Tourism has
become the noblest instrument of this century for achieving international understanding. It enables contacts among people from the most
distant parts of the globe, people of various languages, race, creed,
political beliefs and economic standing. Tourism brings them together,
it is instrumental in their dialogue, it leads to personal contact in which

people can understand attitudes and beliefs which were incomprehensible to them because they were distant. In this way it helps to bridge gaps and erase differences. Since its focal point is man and not the economy, tourism can be one of the most important means, especially in developing countries, of bringing nations closer together and of maintaining good international relations. This noble task is today more important than ever. It therefore overshadows all other means striving for international friendship.'

This was the theory twenty years ago. Today, when travelling has become a mass phenomenon, the tale of understanding among peoples is nothing more than wishful thinking, although there are people who would like to award tourism the Nobel Prize for Peace. In contrast, there are others who compare its destructive force to that of the atomic bomb. Friedrich Wagner, the veteran of German travel journalism, famous for his balanced arguments believes it is naive to expect millions of tourists to make friends and spend their time exchanging addresses with the local population. But he also argues that the faith in the mission of tourism as promoting international understanding can be supported by a great deal of practical evidence.[39]

I do not share this faith nor do I know many positive experiences and examples. On the contrary, I believe that the chances for real human contact between holiday-makers and locals could hardly be less hopeful. The contact is usually only skin-deep, the relationship a mere illusion. Where the main reason for travelling is to get away from things, where the tourist ignores the existence of other people; where assembly line techniques are the only way of dealing with huge numbers, where profit making rules supreme, where there are feelings of superiority and inferiority, there the heart must lose and no communication can develop. This does not apply only to tourism in less developed countries. When citizens of the industrial nations travel within their own countries, the brief contact they have with each other seldom produces real understanding and communication.

Black prospects for meaningful contact

It is often forgotten that tourists and natives are in diametrically opposite situations. What is freedom and pleasure for the former, means burden and work for the latter. Leisure time behaviour clashes with work behaviour, recreational needs with existential ones; one person's money is the other person's bread. How can people who live off tourism be blamed if they are more interested in the money and less in the person? Natives in continuous contact with tourists soon discover their weaknesses and uncertainties in a strange environment. Some of them exploit it, others develop feelings of contempt.

Travellers too have an egoistic attitude. The one thing they care about is their recreation. They are not really interested in meeting the natives, unless it can contribute to their entertainment and add variety to the trip. Thus both parties, the tourists and the locals, keep at a safe distance from each other. True, 75 per cent of the locals interviewed in a Swiss resort described their relations with tourists as friendly and only 25 per cent as reserved.[40] But even the sociologists who conducted the study believe this 'friendly' attitude to be largely caused by a commercial interest in tourists, who are regarded by the locals as a 'precious commodity'. The same study found a particularly positive attitude to tourists in the older generation of natives, which comes from the experiences of 'individual tourism' and personal contact with their (regular) guests. The attitudes of the younger generation have been shaped to a much greater extent by the mass tourism that has developed in the meantime. The locals in this village make a definite linguistic difference between 'tourists' and 'guests': the term 'guest' carries the connotation of a friendly and personal relationship. Guests are obviously visitors who stay longer, return to the same place, they are people one knows. Tourists, on the other hand, are the many others: those who stay only a few days, people out for the day, weekend sportsmen. Though an economically important group, they are nothing more than 'merchandise', and once again we see that it is the massivity of tourism and the rationalized and standardized processes it depends on that stand in the way of friendly relations and meaningful communication between travellers and natives. As it is, their contacts never go beyond a mercenary smile and sterile politeness. And when a traveller looks for more, he most often forgets that what is a unique experience for him is, for the native, the umpteenth repetition of the same situation: the same excursions, the same sights, the same festivals and the same questions – from a new batch of tourists, hundreds, thousands of them. The spontaneity gradually wears off – in the farmer whose meadow is crossed daily by dozens of hikers, in the skilift attendant, who has to pass the bar to hundreds of skiers every hour; in the skiing instructor, who must have a party with a group every week; in landlords, hotel and restaurant personnel, in travel guides who meet thousands of guests during the course of the year. They are expected to be eager to talk with the guests, show a smiling face, be polite and helpful – all the time. But many natives are oversaturated with contacts and sooner or later the symptoms of overkill will come to the surface. The overstressed native withdraws or reacts in an irritated and aggressive way. This explains why the local population probably feels even less inclined to establish contact with their visitors than vice versa. What is more, tourist facilities are unsuitable for a meeting: being designed for tourists, they are often unpopular with the locals. Furthermore, their prices may be too high or the presence of natives may be undesirable and even prohibited. The result is segregation instead of integration. The village pub for the native, the house of the guest for the tourist – everyone in their place.

Conditions for an inter-cultural dialogue are even less favourable when the rich travel to the countries of the poor. Behaviour researchers and our own experience teach us that a true meeting is possible only when people have something in common. Where absolutely nothing is shared and where roles are so totally different, no meaningful dialogue can take place.[41] Visitors to the Third World and natives belong not only to different cultures but to different social classes. The difference couldn't be greater for the haves have come to the have-nots. In order to lessen the cultural shock and ensure a relaxing holiday, tourists are fenced off from the host country and its people in ghettos, the style of which they are familiar with. The direct contact with locals in the promised advertising is arranged on trips in air-conditioned buses, under the protection of the tourist guide, in the comforting bosom of the group. What should have been a meeting becomes a 'zoo syndrome', in which both sides gape at each other. The native becomes an exhibit to be photographed. There is also the language barrier. And since tourists are always pressed for time – one would like to see as much as possible in order to get value for the high price of the trip – there is no opportunity for lingering or quiet observation. Agreed, there are natives in the hotel and on the beach, but they are all some kind of servants: waiters, chambermaids, guards, souvenir sellers, drivers, musicians, folk dancers. This reinforces the feeling of one's own superiority.[42] Two authors from Third World countries describe it in the following way: 'He (the tourist) comes actually because of the country and not because of the people. He is a passer-by who doesn't see the country as it really is. What he wants to find is only a confirmation of his preconceived ideas of the holiday; namely, all the comfort he is used to and a country that exists in his imagination.'[43] And: 'It is not a country they visit, it is the phantom of a country – where their attention is drawn only by what is unusual, bizarre, overwhelming or minute. The hurried tour shows only what the traveller had expected. In this it is almost impossible to avoid the temptation of ethnocentrism, i.e. of a nationalism in which one's own culture is the only standard.'[44] Do not many of the things described here apply also to tourism in our own countries?

The glasses of prejudice

No wonder, then, that travel in its current form hardly helps to bring people closer together and promote their mutual understanding. The dim glasses of prejudice are never taken off. Although there are studies of the subject, all indications are that travel, especially to countries with a totally different culture, does not diminish prejudice but reinforces it. The other people are poor but happy. Carefree, easy-going, and hospitable, but yes, a bit untidy, not so clean you understand, yes, even dirty and unhygienic, certainly unreliable, lazy too, and, well, not so very intelligent. Well, that's exactly what one had expected, it's not surprising, that's what Africa's like – people say. Or: Well, you know, typically Italian, or French, or German, or whatever. The image we have of other nationalities is as distorted as their image of ourselves. For the native, the tourist's behaviour is typical of his country. In his eyes, for example, tourists are immensely rich and never have to work. 'Tourists are people who visit islands to celebrate festivals.' Or because they walk around half-naked, they must come from 'cold islands'. 'In the cold parts they cannot go to the beach because snow is falling and certain parts of the beach is frozen.' These are quotations from children's essays.[45] Neither the native nor the tourist know what their respective worlds are really like. In this way travel confirms the clichés of both host and guest.

Misunderstanding instead of understanding among peoples. At times confrontation instead of meeting. In the worst case mutual contempt instead of esteem: tourists despise the 'underdeveloped' natives, and natives in their turn despise the unrestrained foreigners. But, again, we should not generalize because we do not know enough about this area. One thing is however certain: tourists and natives come nowhere near a meaningful contact – far from it, in fact.

8

The return and the feedback

Recuperated?

'Relaxation is the incentive and reason for travelling, but seldom its effect . . . People have enough time during the year to recuperate from the last trip for the next.'[46] Ironic but true: the holidays and the weekend do not bring urgently needed physical and mental relaxation. On the contrary, the stress involved in holidays and leisure time is considerable. Medical experts who have studied the problem report that the great majority of 'normal holiday-makers' do not return home relaxed and refreshed but tense, nervous and distracted.[47] One psychiatrist has observed what he calls a 'holiday syndrome' in many holiday-makers on their return home, manifesting itself in insomnia, exhaustion and anxiety. They need medical help to return to normal life.[48] And who hasn't heard people complain about the fact that only a few weeks after the holidays they feel their effect has already worn off?

Doctors tell us that relaxation can set in only if we give our body time to adapt to the new situation. We should follow a three-step scheme: rest – relaxation – recuperation. The first three days should be reserved for rest, the third day being the most critical from the medical point of view. If we don't do this properly, apparently we are in great danger of suffering some psychological disturbance ranging from prolonged irritation to a breakdown or other crisis. It is only after these three days that the body is ready: recuperation can begin. Physicians also recommend holidays lasting at least three successive weeks. The 'recuperation peak' usually comes during the third week – but it does not exclude a sudden drop of form on returning home.[49]

The average tourist, however, tosses this advice to the winds and does everything that is harmful from the medical point of view. Instead of gliding leisurely into the holidays, he or she rushes headlong into the holiday turmoil: from the constant stress of the daily round to the stress of holiday-making via the shortest route; from one kind of tension into another; covering thousands of kilometres in a few hours to get from one climate into another. Everything is done at the same hectic pace as during the rest of the year at home. People want to make the best of it, embrace the whole world, get a nice tan and be on top form as soon as possible. They also want to eat, drink and be merry. And thus it all ends up in what is practically a holiday race. Taking it easy, resting and meditating, passing into a state of timelessness, switching off and just being lazy – this is a feat very few people succeed in accomplishing. Where more and more people seek relaxation, fewer and fewer of them really find it. Then there's another thing: when on holiday, things have to be done so that others can be told about it afterwards. 'I did nothing' does not sound serious enough. 'The vacation is the continuation of work by other means.'[50] The exertions are overwhelming. People live consciously or unconsciously against their biological rhythm: they force themselves to relax until they collapse from the effort. And then suddenly, it all becomes too much, one has overdone it and has sunburn, a headache, an upset stomach, a row with the husband, the wife, the children, or with the neighbours on the beach or the camping site.[51] Not infrequently there are additional irritations: long queues, mile-long traffic jams, engine trouble; strikes by customs officers, ground-control personnel, hotel staff, overbooked hotels and camping sites, bad weather, dirty beaches, lousy food. Many millions of holiday-makers are plagued by the so-called 'la Turista', i.e. digestive problems developed while travelling. When the holiday-maker returns home, what he needs is . . . a holiday.

These are the reasons why more and more doctors advocate a 'holiday from the holiday' and suggest an adaptation interval of two to three days before going back to work. Even the weekend can be harmful according to doctors specializing in leisure time. Rushing from one stimulus to another, from one kind of tension to another, merely produces negative effects.[52] And don't we all know them? – the Monday blues. What is needed, apparently, is a recovery period. We are not tired because we have to work again but because the weekend was tiring. The critical third day . . .

Happy and content?

If not fully rested, are people at least satisfied with their trip, have they brought home some happiness, are they more content than before? After all, this may be more important both for the individual person and for society than mere rest and relaxation. These questions, however, cannot be answered by a simple yes or no. True, a number of studies on tourist satisfaction have been undertaken. One of the questions tourists were asked was: 'When you think about it now: how satisfied were you with your holiday?' 90 per cent of travellers say they were satisfied, 50 per cent say they had very good holidays, 40 per cent say they had good holidays.[53] The satisfaction quota is obviously very high and has varied very little over the years. Nothing but sunshine then? At least two points have to be made here. As we have seen, people have a whole bag full of wishes and longings that they associate with holidays. Many of their expectations, however, are general and somewhat vague. Since they are not asked to be specific about what they were satisfied or dissatisfied with – the accommodation, the food, the weather, the partners, the entertainment, the sights – their answer must, in fact, be positive. There must be something they liked, and even if there wasn't, they didn't have to work. And this is very important – many people may be satisfied with their holiday for no other reason than that of not having to work. Apart from this, they have no particular demands!

The second objection is even more important, and is in agreement with the findings of all leisure time psychologists: few people can admit to themselves, or to others, that their holidays were disappointing.[54] They simply must have been a success because they are what one had worked for, had been looking forward to and had chosen from among many other possibilities. After all, if everybody else has had a wonderful vacation, how can one admit that one's own did not live up to expectations: that Togo was in fact too hot, or that the hot sex life in Bangkok was only lukewarm. Everybody, then, plays the role of the happy holiday-maker. To admit that the holiday was less than 'wonderful' is unthinkable – it would be tantamount to social failure. Thus disappointments are treated differently to those in everyday life: they are either suppressed or made light of. They may even be refurbished into adventures and special experiences, as Paul Rieger points out. This is how he describes the phenomenon:[55]

> The funny thing about it is that shattered illusions are practically never passed on. People keep these to themselves. Back among his colleagues and relatives, the first question the disappointed person will be asked is: 'How was your holiday?' and then he will spin the yarn to an audience who are as used to clichés and stereotypes as the narrator himself. What else could he tell them? Wouldn't he discredit himself if he admitted that there had been nothing, no adventure, just a bit of wrapping and some tinsel? No, he can't risk telling the truth! Instead, he describes the

holiday in rosy terms and it is only then that it becomes really enjoyable. He tells his listeners it was simply terrific. They listen full of admiration and perhaps some envy and decide silently they too will go there next year . . . A lot of holiday ballyhoo is nothing but showing off.

Even if we cannot present hard facts about travel satisfaction, one thing is certain: when people travel, they experience more freedom, have more contact with nature and with other people and generally have a more interesting time than usual. All of these things represent a gain compared to normal life and can help reduce life's shortcomings at least temporarily. Indeed, it is not 'the experience of a lifetime', nor great and profound emotions, but the little things, the many brief moments of happiness that produce the feeling of satisfaction during the holidays.[56] The smallest pleasures – some sunshine, a little laughter, nice people, some exercise and fresh air are often enough to do the job.

Equally certain is the fact that travel and holidays can never live up to the excessive expectations, idealistic images, and desires that many people project on them. The few weeks spent on holiday should bring a fountain of youth which will regenerate the overstressed nerves, firm the flabby muscles, offer active experiences, and self-realization, satisfy the thirst for togetherness and new contacts, help in overcoming loneliness, rebuild or heal broken marriages, and so on and so forth. A great festival of freedom and happiness celebrated in a paradise. Even the most beautiful holiday must necessarily fall short of these exaggerated expectations. The holiday world is never as beautiful as it appears in the tourist brochures. Most people soon become aware of the fact that the emptiness of everyday life cannot be filled by a few short moments of creative leisure or a little extra freedom during one's holidays. Consequently people content themselves with what the holidays have brought . . . and no sooner back home, look forward to the next time. There were many more things they wanted to see and do but the time was so short. The next holidays, though, will surely be different. Such unfulfilled and keenly felt needs keep the pot of travelling on the boil. The cycle can begin once again.

Let us now come to the most important point of this analysis: what travel and holidays bring to the individual person, what benefit he can derive from them, depends less on what happens in the holidays than it does on everyday life. People who are generally happy and satisfied, who have enough room and possibilities for self-fulfilment, people who have succeeded in escaping from the continuous stress of isolation and who have stimulating contacts and relationships with other people, do not need holidays or travel to escape or compensate for what they miss in life. For them holidays can be a truly enriching time, because they are not frustrated and worn out by everyday life and therefore have a surplus of energy and interests. They are ready to turn to other things, take up other activities, explore and learn. They can truly benefit from their holidays and draw inspiration from them for a long time. People who cannot find self-realization at home, won't find it during the holidays either. The four or so weeks just won't do the magic trick of producing emancipation. Things that do not work in everyday life cannot suddenly function on holiday. People who are generally communicative, will also find friends on vacation. Sensitive people will be impressed by beautiful scenery and respond to the charm of another person much sooner than unresponsive people. Imaginative, creative and dynamic persons will have a genuine holiday of discovery.[57]

What is left? – travelling as learning and exploration

What do people take home from their travels? Are the souvenirs placed on the bookshelf or hung on the wall or the photographs in the album the only durable memories? Or do they undergo enriching experiences, does the holiday perhaps even help them to change their attitudes and behaviour?

There are two theories about this. One of them says that with no time to reflect upon our impressions the daily routine soon obliterates all the after-effects of the holiday, and that soon we are its prisoners again. The fact that we have to go back to work is felt to be the natural course of events. The holidays are the cake of the year, the three-week-illumination. This is probably the attitude of most holiday-makers. They need the holidays in order to have a break and to be able to go on. They have got used to this rhythm and the corresponding behaviour patterns so much that they like the return home. After all, it has always been this way, and home is best – even though this 'best' is often not really very attractive.

The other theory says that it is just as possible that the experiences given by travel and holidays trigger off a learning process which, in the course of time, i.e. as more travel produces further changes in attitudes and behaviour, produce social changes. According to this view, we should not use our experiences just as interesting anecdotes to amuse our friends with, but learn from them and try to apply them. We could learn, for example, from the Latin American sociologist who recommends that:[58] 'We work just enough to earn as much as we consider necessary to enjoy life. Free time is usually valued much more than overtime pay. We cannot teach you how to work, but we may have some good suggestions about how to relax.' This sounds almost like the advice of a German tour guide to his guests: 'What we should learn from Latin Americans is their imperturbability, cheerfulness and mañana-thinking – the very things we lay at their door as faults.'

Johann Wolfgang von Goethe wrote 200 years ago: 'I have so often observed that when one comes back home, the mind, instead of confining itself according to the circumstances one finds there, would prefer to expand the circumstances to the distance from which one has come, and when this is not possible, one tries to bring and squeeze in as many new ideas as possible, without knowing whether they will go in and fit or not.'[59] According to our second theory travel could help us become aware of our own reality, discover new possibilities for living with other people, and lead us to question the circumstances we live in. It sees travel as a 'school of life'. Travel could indeed bring all these things. But as long as it remains what most of it is today, namely a commercially organized, unproblematic consumer pleasure for the citizens of the industrialized countries, its great potential will continue to be largely unexploited or at best will be tapped only by a small minority of enlightened people, although they could form an important vanguard for the masses of people who may one day follow suit. Indeed, many things ought to be changed in the 'tourism system' if the tourist leisure world is to become a learning ground, a testing ground and a practice ground. Exploratory behaviour during the holidays is facilitated by the change of roles. Alternative forms of life can be practised in a free and easy-going atmosphere. This aspect of travel is becoming increasingly important for young people. The holidays can be the chance to learn to be free and independent, find a new meaning to life, and discover new things. Travel offers many opportunities. But, as we have already said, such opportunities persist as theories if travel remains what it is today.

9

Indications for a more critical understanding of tourism

Today tourism is not viewed in the same way as it was in the past, but it is surprising how long the process took and what had to happen for more critical attitudes to develop. Let us think only a short time back: just ten or so years ago – the age of modern mass tourism was already well-established and the problems were already piling up – people involved in tourism had no misgivings about the phenomenon of travel. The 1960s saw the beginning of a universal and unrestrained tourist development euphoria. More and more countries, regions and businesses tried to grab a share of the bonanza of the century. They viewed the tourist business as the great chance, the well-deserved compensation for the lean years of crisis and war, the long-awaited possibility to set economic development going or to acquire for themselves a share of the foreign exchange injected by tourists into their countries. In the rare cases when the effects of this development were analysed at all, the studies were limited to purely economic considerations. The euphoria was bound to be followed by disenchantment. In the early 1970s, it became clear that the spirits that had been invoked were now demanding their tribute and that it would not be at all easy to get rid of them. The landscape eaters and the all too obvious effects of tourism on the environment, had become an issue of public debate. Thus, it is only comparatively recently that discussions have turned to the area of problems which should have been studied before everything else and which is the topic of this book: namely the psychological and social effects of tourism. Not only its own fast rate of growth but also the general changes in social structure and social consciousness have led to a new awareness about such effects. There is a new criticism aimed at tourism that cannot be easily dismissed. The new doubts express an unease about the various phenomena of industrial society. The debate has focused on the effects caused by tourism as a product of the industrialized society. There are now worldwide discussions about the cost and benefit of tourism to the economy, environment and society, whereas earlier all that was ever mentioned was the benefit and the economy. The questions are now discussed by many people and not just by a few theoreticians concerned with the carrying capacity of recreational areas and of the people living there. Tourism and its various aspects has become the favourite subject of debate and study of numerous international organizations, congresses, seminars and symposia. The matter has aroused much negative criticism, as can be seen from a sample of titles of TV films and programmes shown recently in Germany, Austria and Switzerland:

'*The Alps-Apocalypse*'
'*The Poisoned Snow – The Winter Sports Business*'
'*Is Tourism Ruining Land and People?*'
'*Tourists and Locals – Meeting or Confrontation?*'
'*Adventure as a Consumer Commodity – Tourism in the Third World*'
'*Tourism – A New Form of Colonialism?*'

Most importantly, these questions are now also being raised in numerous tourist destination areas where attitudes have been changing.

The 'rebellion of the hosts' or: the awakened self-confidence of the local population

In quite a number of the popular travel destinations the local population is viewing the tourist boom with growing unease. A critical awareness is already very articulate in some traditional tourist areas and is gaining ground in developing countries as well. What may be called 'the rebellion of the hosts' manifests itself initially mostly in individual signs of protest or spontaneous defence reactions. It is only at a later stage that the resistance gets organized, giving birth to political groups demanding moderation and self-determination in the development of tourism.

Here are a few examples of the worldwide awakening of local sensitivity to what is seen by many as unfeeling and rampant tourist development:

When in the late 1970s the great shopping-tourist wave swept over London, one could see some Londoners wearing T-shirts with the printed message 'I am not a tourist'. The famous playwright John Osborne (*Look Back in Anger*) published a sensational feature story in the *Evening Standard*, in which he described London as an enormous tourist slum and offered his harassed fellow-countrymen a number of 'solutions': 'Tourists, whether they be Americans, Germans (especially), Japanese (perhaps most of all), even the biggest nation of geniuses in the world – the Italians, all are human garbage. . . . Make it as uncomfortable and unwelcoming as possible. . . . Your first greeting from a lonely and isolated Australian is "Why are you here?" Your second "When are you leaving?" . . . Be like the French, refuse to be polite, answer no questions and speak no language but your own and then pretend not to understand their appalling syntax.'[60]

In the Scandinavian countries, Sweden, Norway and Finland, reservations about the unlimited influx of foreign visitors have been voiced for a long time now. This has led, among other things, to the slogan 'Sweden for Swedes' and to a cut in the funds for the advertising of tourism abroad. At a conference in Jutland, tourist experts, politicians and environmentalists all agreed about one thing in an unanimously adopted resolution: 'Neither nature nor people can take more tourists', and a mayor warned the tourist experts: 'You must not expand the trade to such an extent that no room is left for us! We don't want our people to have to dress up in old folk costumes for the sake of tourists!'[61]

In Switzerland an obvious and growing resistence of the local population to tourism at all costs can be observed in many areas. In well-known holiday areas and resorts projects aimed at bringing in more tourist businesses have been rejected in referenda. People, and especially the young, have been setting up committees, associations, working parties and activist groups and fighting against large-scale tourist projects and the building on of open land, and trying to promote harmonious development without destruction. This resistance is slowly giving rise to positive concepts for a different tourism, which are presented to the general public in a number of informative brochures. The activity taking place in the village of Erschmatt in Valais is illustrative of many similar initiatives and shows what the new intentions are.

Here is an extract from the statute of the Pro Erschmatt Society:[62]

> The Pro Erschmatt Society sees tourism as a possibility for development of the village. This can have its advantages and its drawbacks, it can work for the village and its population, or against it. For this reason, the

People under stress – harnessed day in, day out, by the same alienating and automated work processes, where the end of the working day, the weekend and the holidays provide the only hope and where better life is a dream . . .

. . . a dream of the Garden of Eden, of a life of leisure, of countries where lemon-trees blossom, of a Sunday world without problems and full of happiness . . .

. . . dreams processed by desire factories into advertisements and tied into travel packages, cleverly managed and marketed by paradise-sellers of all kinds. Offers you can't refuse. Holidays described in small works of fiction.

Holidays must make dreams come true: Who doesn't want . . .

. . . to move freely in nature, test and improve their fitness, relax, preferably at some distance from the crowded tourist scene, although not too far away . . .

. . . escape from isolation, be with nice people, make new friends, rediscover childlike enthusiasms, play, have fun, frolic . . .

. . . let off steam, rediscover the family, one's partner, the children, joke, laugh, discuss, make love, fill up on life . . .

Just remember that while on holiday and away from home, I am an exceptional person and I do things I would never do normally. I want to be a pasha for a few days, give orders, be pampered by others, behave as I please. I'm not interested in what people will say. I've paid for this! And tomorrow I'll be gone anyway.

The cliché image of tourists. There is hardly a category of people more laughed at or ridiculed. And tourists are never ourselves.

The 'Clubs' as self-sufficient holiday complexes. Designed and run,
on the basis of careful motivation studies, as enclaves for holiday-
makers. Total experience and relaxation. Fenced off and sterilized.

The famous Club buffets: 'la grande bouffe' as a holiday attraction.
Gourmandize until you burst at the seams. Who cares if other
people go hungry. Nobody has a bad conscience on holiday.

I am a water-nymph and would like to have a five-mile beach all to myself. What do I find in Aldiana? A fifteen-mile beach – fortunately not all to myself.

Please don't ask me how many times I've taken a swim while water-skiing today. But you can ask me how I have managed to become the Club champion in backgammon and clay pigeon shooting!

I love the free and cheerful Club atmosphere. I look forward to it 335 days of the year. The day after I've returned from my holiday, I'm homesick for Aldiana again.

I've learned German at the Club. And Marathon serving.

Such a terrific holiday with the nice set is the absolute tops. If you want company, you'll never be alone – not at the pool games, not on excursions and certainly not in the discotheque.

At the Club I can windsurf for miles: there are enough boards for professionals and beginners can take a course here. In the evening I surf at

Aldiana Club. Where happy people spend their holiday.

Why do I spend my vacation only with Aldiana? Because two years ago I happened to get into this lot of happy people. Happiness is catching!

I want to scubadive to my heart's content without continually bumping into someone. And when I surface I want to go sailing, horse riding and dancing, and enjoy myself.

At home I'm too busy to do anything about my fitness. But here at the Club! I'm active all day, I have a terrific time, I can relax and feel I'm on top form.

Twins always come together – and while Ingrid goes diving, I play tennis. I find the right types here for a tough game.

Have you ever ridden for miles across the savanna? You see, that's why I'm here. And because the Club restaurant is really first class.

At Aldiana there is a children's club and our Christine has as much fun and as many friends there as we at the 'big' club. We live in a very chic family bungalow.

Alternative travelling: off the beaten track, under the protective wing of the group. Adventure at catalogue prices and with a hot shower in the evening.

. . . or on an entirely private discovery tour. Engine trouble in the desert – a new experience. Next year there will certainly be a desert road here, a desert hotel and an air conditioned bus instead of the jeep.

Pro Erschmatt Society supports a healthy tourism adapted to local needs meeting the following criteria:

- It must benefit the population as a whole and not individual speculators;
- It must not abuse the environment – our capital – through speculation and thereby rob it of its recreational quality, but respect both the landscape and village architecture;
- It must take into account future generations and be based on medium and long-term solutions, rather than on short-term ones;
- It should allow the community to develop and should not impose a prohibitive infrastructural burden on it;
- It should not involve speculation leading to rocketing land prices, which make property too expensive for the local population;
- It should not lead to a sell-out of our country;
- It must not generate dead holiday villages, inhabited for only a few weeks in the year;
- It must be based on autonomous local decision making, i.e. on equal participation of the local population in the planning and realization of tourist projects;
- It must create attractive jobs, take into account the local businesses and not waste building land.

An increasing number of people realize that a one-legged economy, based only on tourism, is more prone to crisis than a well-balanced one. Therefore, alternatives to tourist development are being sought with a new intensity – for instance within the framework of a comprehensive national research programme in Switzerland.[63] The arguments in favour of the preservation and improvement of agriculture are undergoing a revival.

Travelling in Third World countries has become the target of especially vehement criticism. Growing concern about the grave social and cultural consequences of the tourism of the rich in the countries of the poor has, in recent years, brought about worldwide anti-tourist movement. In many countries – especially in Europe and the USA – there are now many groups critical of tourism. They hold their own international seminars – anti-conferences to the official congresses on tourism.[64] They publish books and documents,[65] bring out informative booklets for tourists,[66] organize exhibitions, have their own magazines.[67] Charity organizations, the Church and young intellectuals are particularly active in these groups. The aim of most members of this movement, which must be taken very seriously, is not to abolish tourism altogether, but rather to look for alternative forms of travel. At the moment, however, positive action is still lagging behind verbal criticism. Due to their hard line towards official and commercial tourism, the groups run the risk of being pushed aside and in the end achieve very little. Their cause would probably be better served by an attempt to co-operate. It is however very significant that more and more affected locals from tourist target areas are joining the movement. True, they are still only a small minority. But one thing is certain: there are increasing signs of annoyance about certain effects of tourism and an ever louder clamour for counter-measures, even from influential quarters. The critics can consider this a success. For instance, not long ago several Kenyan newspapers sharply criticized the behaviour of European tourists in their country. The Nairobi *Sunday Standard* wrote: 'The invaders of today do not come with canon or swords. They come with drugs, money and strange customs.' It urged the authorities to do something before the situation gets totally out of control.[68] Similar complaints about lax and inconsiderate behaviour of tourists can be heard in Sri Lanka. The Minister for Tourism has demanded strict measures against tourists who shock the native population and offend the good manners of the country by engaging in prostitution, drug abuse, nudism and the like. What hurts the Ceylonese feelings most is the lack of respect tourists display in temples and on historical sites. They have no qualms about clicking their cameras where it is forbidden to take pictures, and think nothing of scrambling over altars, graves and monuments and scratching the date of their visit on statues of Buddha. Commenting on this vandalism, one local politician said (probably quite rightly) that visitors from the West would almost certainly not do anything of the kind in a cathedral in Rome or a museum in London or Paris.[69] There is growing concern among tourist experts in Third World countries, who are increasingly looking for an acceptable solution to the dilemma of how to extract as many dollars as possible from the pockets of holiday-makers without becoming a nation of servants, toads and crooks.

These and many other examples are evidence of the emergence of a new, differentiated foreign tourism policy in many tourist areas around the world. In the course of this development the host population will make increasing efforts to regain their autonomy in deciding about essential matters and not leave them to outsiders. Eventually they will take the market dictates from the hands of the foreign tourist entrepreneurs. There is a growing readiness to change the scale of excessive development targets and introduce safeguards against the unwanted effects of tourism. The terms and guarantees attached to tourist development will become more numerous and restrictive. This is not to say however that a change for the better is apparent everywhere. Despite all the warnings, reckless land development by tourist entrepreneurs is continuing in many areas, following the familiar patterns sanctioned by a complacent market. Out of sheer ignorance or against better judgement, the same mistakes are being made over and over again. People simply will not learn from the frightening examples that can be seen all over the world – perhaps because the places where they have been made are still relatively successful on the market and because there have so far been no spectacular breakdowns which would have triggered off a reaction on a international scale. Nevertheless I am convinced that the native population in host areas is becoming increasingly aware of tourist-related problems and that they are prepared to put up a fight to save their own values. In the long-term, new forms of tourism will be – will have to be – developed everywhere. But whether the turning point may come too late for many areas remains an open question.

From the manipulated to the emancipated tourist

The second factor which could fundamentally change tourism are tourists themselves. Unlike cultural pessimists and social critics, who are often bitingly sarcastic about the search of happiness and liberation in tourism and who call it a mere illusion, I am an optimist: I believe that the emancipation of tourists is possible – even though the process of learning and growing up that travellers will have to go through cannot take place overnight. It will require time, patience and education, just like the emancipation of their hosts. The well-known hierarchy of motives proposed by the US psychologist A. H. Maslow could very well be applied to tourism, because the development of tourist needs in the course of time is very similar to the development of human needs in general. Maslow suggested a five-step pyramid of needs which every person tries to climb. Step 1: the satisfaction of physiological needs; step 2: the need for safety; step 3: the need for a sense of belonging and love; 4: the need for esteem; step 5: the need for self-realization and self-development. When the needs of one step have been satisfied, they are replaced by those of the step above.

I am convinced that the progressive development of tourist needs is based on this inner organization. This means that we shall increasingly see emancipated tourists, tourists who have, so to speak, come of age. Their need for physical recreation (sleeping, eating, drinking) will decline in favour of the need for 'emotional recreation' through activities and experiences which are not possible in everyday life. Many tourists are becoming more demanding. They take the satisfaction of their elementary needs, for instance good food and comfortable lodging, more or less, for granted. What they want to find now, in addition to this, is the satisfaction of social needs: contact with other people and self-realization through creative activities, knowledge and exploration. They are no longer interested only in culinary pleasures but also in intellectual pleasures. The search is now going in the direction of continuous sophistication and refinement of recreational needs, which can be described as 'the birth of a new travel culture'. Indeed, there are many new characteristics in our society which may help to accelerate this change: the striving for independence and individuality coupled with an increasing awareness of the importance of immaterial values such as health, the environment, nature, knowledge and education. It is a development away from a manipulated tourist to an informed and experienced one to an emancipated and independent tourist, a critical consumer not only at home but also when travelling. A new tourist, who clearly expresses his needs and behaves accordingly. And this implies that what up to now has been a sellers' market will be replaced by a buyers' market – a market in which the consumer has the say and not the producer.

Admittedly, what may sound convincing in theory is still far from reality. Passive and uncritical tourists still far outnumber active and enlightened ones. But the readiness and desire for a different tourism is becoming more widespread day by day.

PART THREE

For a humanization of everyday life

Let us imagine that the enormous sums of money spent every year on travelling for pleasure were used for the embellishment of our cities and landscapes, the improvement of our work places, the search for a harmonious life! Let us imagine that the charm and beauty of holidays could trickle into everyday life! Then all the problems of tiredness and the need for recuperation would be solved by what I propose to call the 'solution of the heart'. No more holidays or – if you like – endless holidays. True life, genuine happiness. . . .

Michel Tournier

10

Everyday life in working society – work, home and leisure time in a bottleneck

Beginning with everyday life, we want to show what happens at work, at home and during our leisure time, and indicate where the opportunities for change exist. Then we propose to consider what measures could be taken for improving travel. What interests us, then, is not only how we may add new perspectives to travel and holidays, but also how our day-to-day existence may be modified so that life in general may become more satisfying and meaningful. To make that which is felt to be the counter-world a natural part of social reality,[1] to have, in short, more holiday in everyday life.

The working society heading for crisis

What does work mean to man? Modern industrial psychology tells us that man has a very complex attitude to work. We can observe some elements of this complex relationship in ourselves: work is indispensable to secure the necessities of life, it is a way of earning money; it is toil and exertion. But work also enables us to be productive and creative, to enrich our lives, to broaden our horizons. Self-esteem, respect, pride, self-development and self-realization are all closely connected with work. But work in the modern industrial world cannot satisfy all these needs and the possibility for it to do so is becoming more and more remote.

All human history has been a history of work. In early times work was regarded as a curse and a burden. 'In the sweat of your face you shall eat bread ...' Then came the Reformers, who preached that work was a vocation and that it gave man dignity: 'Make the soil your servant'. A new ethos was born – the Protestant Work Ethic; its basic principles were the will to work, efficiency, a sense of order, diligence and discipline.[2] This positive attitude to work ultimately led to the dynamic system of our present-day industrial society – a system based on economic efficiency and technological rationality. Ours is a society of achievement, competition and success; its value system is based on material wealth.[3] It is a society in which work is identified with progress and prosperity, in which education and training are job-oriented, in which free time is reserved for relaxation and consumption and retirement is regarded as a well-earned reward for a lifetime of hard work.

The development of industrial society has produced the long-desired affluence and eliminated poverty. The two main social achievements of this progress have been higher wages and shorter working hours and these yardsticks of prosperity have become the credo of industrial society. Indeed, their annual growth rates are used to measure progress. The results that have been achieved are spectacular: while in the 18th and the early 19th centuries the mass of the population worked 4000 to 4500 hours per year – some people working a seven-day week and a fifteen-hour day – in industrialized countries today people work between 1700 and 2100 hours per year.[4] The increase in leisure time has likewise been impressive. While in the period between 1900 and 1940 about 75 per cent of the achieved increase in productivity went into shorter working hours, between 1940 and 1980 around 80 to 90 per cent of it was used for wage increases.[5] In Switzerland, the per capita disposable real income has more than doubled since 1950 and in the Federal Republic of Germany, it has even quadrupled.[6] So much for the undeniable achievements – a progress which nobody would like to give up. But there is a reverse side to the coin and it shows the negative aspects of industrial development. Although many politicians bury their heads in the sand before the facts, they cannot be got rid of by mere talking. They are rapidly getting out of hand, and if nothing is done to prevent them, will take us – rather like an express train – into a long black tunnel with a dead end.

Negative aspect 1: Loss of the sense of purpose and responsibility at work

Mass production and a strict division of labour reinforced by new technologies and the latest production processes, are reducing jobs into ever smaller and more specialized sub-tasks. Many people are becoming increasingly alienated from their work, the result being a totally automatic performance, a chore in which content and purpose have been replaced by money.

Negative aspect 2: Diminishing job satisfaction and as a result less satisfaction with life in general

Studies show that three-quarters of those who find complete satisfaction in their work are also satisfied with their lives.[7] However, a growing number of people are increasingly dissatisfied with their jobs. In Germany only 18 per cent of the working population declare they are satisfied with what they do[8] and about half of all men in Germany see no opportunity for self-realization.[9] Despite more money and less work, the general sense of well-being seems to be diminishing.

Negative aspect 3: Rigid schedules and time drill

The need to keep to working hours has imposed a rigid pattern on life as a whole. There are strict rules about when work is to begin, when it can be interrupted for a break, and when it ends. This goes on day after day, week after week. The time scale must be the same for everybody, the work coming in tightly sealed, standardized packets. There is no room for free decisions. Now it is machines and not the rhythm of man and nature that determine how our time is broken up. It is all a time drill with clock-chasing, shrill sirens, digital clocks, clocking-in cards, clock-watching and finally home again for dinner on the dot.

Negative aspect 4: Leisure time is time left over after work

Shorter working hours have given people more free time, but even that free time is determined and influenced by work. Leisure time is a remainder, a by-product left over from occupational activity. Seen as an independent part of time, it is socially unproductive and hence lacking in purpose or value. Its main and socially accepted use is to serve work: to regenerate man's physical and mental capacity for work. Moreover, leisure time is consumer time creating work and bringing in revenue. And finally, leisure time can be used for educational purposes – again preferably to further one's progress in the world of work.

Negative aspect 5: Stress and boredom at work and at leisure

The automated and specialized work environment is the cause of increasing stress and boredom. People no longer know the whys and wherefors of their work, they cannot understand, influence or control it. But stress is not only the result of overtaxing work situations, which then get out of hand – it can also be produced by situations which under-exploit people's mental or physical abilities.

Modern working conditions have contributed to this kind of stress too. Over 40 per cent of the Swiss labour force complain about being under stress and time pressure at work,[10] while another Swiss survey shows that as many as two-thirds of the working population feel they are under greater stress today than only a few years ago.[11] There is also a growing feeling of boredom during free time: every third German complains of this, while thirty years ago only every fifth person suffered from this kind of problem.[12] Some medical sociologists fear that our lives will become totally 'medicalized' in the not so distant future. The dramatic increase in the consumption of medicines is another result of stress and boredom.

Negative aspect 6: Unemployment – millions without work and social recognition

Since the mid-60s unemployment has spread like a cancerous growth over the industrialized countries. The number of people joining the ranks of the unemployed has been steadily rising, and today in the 1980s, the disease has become rampant mainly because of declining economic growth; the introduction of new technologies which have reduced the need for manpower, and not least because of the increase in the number of people seeking first-time employment (caused primarily by the baby-boom in the 1960s, before the advent of the pill and the professional emancipation of women). Far from coming as a surprise, this development had been predicted a number of years ago.[13] The jobless population in western industrialized countries has, in the meantime, grown to over 30 million. These figures conceal tremendous psychological problems for those affected by unemployment: the feeling of being a failure, of no use, superfluous and rejected by society. The consequences are resignation, bouts of depression, or – especially in the unemployed young – hatred of society, leading to a gradual slide into the world of crime, political extremism, drug abuse or escape into various religious or pseudo-religious sects.

Where work is becoming less and less satisfying, emptier of content and purpose, it is leisure that should bring compensation and the missing satisfaction. Unfortunately, many people spend their leisure in ersatz activities, for their energy and creativity after a working day or week is low. Their financial resources are often too modest to pay for the wide range of ersatz offerings provided by the leisure industry.

The future of a working society in its present form looks bleak. Although the population growth in the industrialized countries has largely come to a standstill, the developing countries will see to it that the world population rises from the current 4.7 billion to 6.4 billion in the year 2000.[14] If we wanted to solve the problem of unemployment on a worldwide scale, we would have to create a thousand million new jobs by the year 1990. In the industrialized countries, the number of young people looking for jobs will increase by another 20 millions by the end of the 1980s.[15] Their chances of finding employment are slim, as already ten million sixteen- to twenty-four-year-olds are unemployed. After the 1990s, it will be the gradual increase in the percentage of elderly people that promises to become one of the biggest headaches of our society. The number of people aged sixty and over – the pensioner brigade – is growing rapidly and the ratio between wage earners and the non-active population is deteriorating just as quickly. Who is going to pay for all the old-age pensions? The current model of life in industrialized society offers no solution for this problem. And what will happen if technical progress continues and the number and quality of jobs decline even further? The super-industrial breakthrough appears to be preprogrammed. We have already entered the microelectronic age. The magazine *Business Week* estimates that in the next two decades 45 per cent of all jobs in the industrialized countries will be altered somehow, or made redundant by microelectronics.[16] In the service sector alone, previously an employment-intensive area, 25 to 30 per cent of office work could be automated.[17] Other experts predict that every second employee in the service sector will become a victim of these 'job killers'. Is it at all conceivable that the people who have been ousted from their jobs by machines could be employed in the production of new machines, as strategists of growth and full employment would have us believe? Vassily Leontief, winner of the Nobel Prize for Economics, has declared that the assumption is equally absurd as the expectation that the horses replaced by motor vehicles could be used in the car industry.[18]

It is a great illusion to believe that the ailing working society could be cured by the old formula 'full employment through economic growth'. Another lasting economic boom cannot be expected – too many things are against it. In addition to the factors we have already mentioned, they include growing production costs due to diminishing resources and expensive technologies, shrinking and partly saturated markets and changing attitudes to work and the economy.[19] It has been estimated that to maintain unemployment at its present level, an annual economic growth of 4 to 5 per cent would be needed, whereas a growth of between 5 and 7 per cent could slightly alleviate unemployment.[20] Yet, all that the industrialized countries can hope to achieve in the 1980s is an average growth rate of 2 to 2.5 per cent – as even the most optimistic experts are forced to admit.

If, under these conditions, we continue to cling to the current structure of industrial working society and particularly to the conventional goal of full employment, then it takes little imagination to see the following picture of a divided future society: a thirty-eight to forty-hour working week with about half the work force doing skilled and well-paid work, the other half having undemanding and unfulfilling jobs and living continually on the brink of unemployment. A third and very distinct group would consist of social dropouts, and the unemployed and underemployed, who would live on a line between legality and crime, unemployment benefit and a black market economy, and whose basic needs would have to be catered for in the same way as for the growing army of the elderly.

The future of our society need not necessarily be this bleak projection of the present. There are other ways out. They will be discussed in a later chapter.

The inhospitable home and the divided life

For many people life means home. People always try to find a niche – it may be a cave or a castle. It is their retreat where they are safe, where they can organize their lives. Home means room, flat, house, front yard, back yard, village, town. Home means sleeping, eating, social contact, leisure, housework, sometimes occupational work as well. The place where we live is of paramount importance because it is there, or near it, that we spend about 60 to 70 per cent of our free time. Its importance is even increasing, for it should also serve as a 'relaxation area', an antidote to the growing stress of work and routine. However, just like the job and the work environment, home cannot satisfy all our wishes, needs and expectations. Indeed, the living conditions in residential areas are continuing to deteriorate instead of improving.

We want to describe some characteristics of modern urban development to show just what has taken place almost everywhere in a matter of a few decades. In earlier centuries the city was the living space in the real sense of the word. There was a harmony between man and architecture. The city was a surveyable whole within chosen boundaries, in which there was room for continuous development employing traditional local building materials and standards. It was a framework whose limits could always be observed. Flats, houses, squares and streets, private, semi-public and public areas stood next to one another in purposeful complementation. The problems began with the emerging industrialization, when the city was suddenly subjected to the requirements of industrial production. The structure of towns was adapted to economic needs and henceforth its development observed only economic principles. The pattern is familiar: work places are concentrated in the centre of the city, and it is there, in the best business locations, that banks, insurance companies, international trade associations, big chain stores and many other strong financial institutions have their buildings. They all fight for property in the city centre, so real estate prices and rents rocket. The residents can no longer afford to live there or only the richest among them can, thus they are gradually ousted from the centre, banned from their neighbourhood, uprooted and thrown out. They must look for a new place to live in the housing estates around the city. Their previous flats are 'improved' and converted into luxury condominiums or office premises: new office blocks are built and the city centre expands, a grey, cold, rational and functional monotony of concrete replacing the former colourful diversity: the city becomes a huge shopping and business centre, shaped by concrete and glass and peopled by always hurrying and alienated crowds. Ever larger city areas are dead after working hours, because their former inhabitants have returned to their dormitories on express motorways or in crowded commuter trains. Only a few decades were needed for western cities to develop into those conglomerates which nobody really wanted. This development has not been determined by the townspeople or by town planning design but by the economy. Planners and designers had nothing against it; on the contrary, they were among the most active advocates of this 'new order'. Already in the 1930s some planners declared that the key to modern urban development lay in the following four functions: home, work, recreation and mobility. Each of these functions was claimed to be autonomous and the best solution was their strict division in space – separate areas for each activity. It is this rational organization that has determined the pattern of our urban development over the past fifty years, a model that has taken into consideration everything except people.

Function 1: Work in the city
Everything is concentrated in city centres, which are totally geared to work – in purpose-built office blocks, factory buildings, canteens, and express restaurants.

Function 2: Housing in agglomerations
These agglomerations grow in concentric circles around a city. Their
stone fingers extend further and further into the countryside, des-
troying its settlements and uprooting its population. They are peopled
by beings living in grey structures resembling silos and bunkers,
separated from one another by easy-to-grow and untouchable green-
ery. Residential buildings designed after machine standards. At the
other end of the housing scale are the sprawling family-house
plantations – to live there, in one's own family house, is almost
everybody's dream and the trend today.

Function 3: Recreation in recreational areas
Since recreation space has not been provided in the residential areas,
because the environment is noisy, built-up or boring, people naturally
want to get away for a time and spend their leisure outdoors –
wherever they can find a bit of free space, nature or a leisure
infrastructure.

Function 4: Mobility
It is mobility that makes it possible. Transportation must ensure the
connection between the three areas of life – work, home and
recreation. Without it the system would break down. It has therefore
been given priority over everything else and its totalitarian demands
must be met. Individual mobility has become a necessity and a right;
mobility means, in the first place, auto-mobility. To this purpose roads
connecting the city, residential areas and recreation areas have been
constructed, bottlenecks have been eliminated and whole tracts of land
cleared in order to facilitate the smooth transit of commuters and
recreation travellers.

   The people-oriented city of the past has been displaced by the
transport-oriented city of modern times. Back yards, gardens, and trees
lining the street have given way to garages, parking lots and two-way
traffic. The grey has ousted the green. Between one-third and one-half
of the area of our cities is reserved for transport in the form of roads
and parking lots instead of being used as living space. The ideal city in
the park has turned into the city in the parking lot. And the
development that began in cities is perpetuating itself outside towns
and in the recreational areas. The Moloch of transport is greedy: it
wants wider roads, more parking space, garages, bridges and tunnels.
Road surfaces are marching on – everywhere.

This is how the development of living and working conditions in industrial society has changed human existence. It has torn man to pieces, broken the harmony of his life and made him homeless. Townspeople have become modern nomads commuting to and fro between the residential area and the city. To and fro, day in, day out, following the French motto: 'auto-métro-boulot-bistro-dodo'. The agglomerations have degenerated into dormitories. 'The agglomerite', as this new type of person is called, lives there in anonymity and is often lonely. He does not feel he belongs to the place, he cannot develop a relationship with it or become involved. His attitude to the city is equally detached. A city user and not a city dweller, he only makes use of the urban work, shopping and recreation facilities. The Swiss writer Peter Bichsel has this to say about it:[21] '. . . who wants to get involved here? W has shifted his allegiance to Crete, Y loves Kenya and X could not live without Italy . . . Our hopes are elsewhere, our friends are elsewhere, our longings have emigrated. We still earn our money here. We still eat and sleep here, and when we can no longer stand it, we go out and eat in a Chinese restaurant.'

So people go out of town and out of the agglomeration as often as possible in order to find 'there' what they miss 'here'. The less attractive the place where they live, the more often do they take to the road. Inhabitants of high-rise blocks and noisy areas go on trips about 30 per cent more often than people living in family houses;[22] the inhabitants of metropolitan areas spend their weekends out of town much more often than the inhabitants of small towns. It is a tragic development: for many people the home is no longer a retreat, a place for the family, leisure, inspiration, communication and contact with nature, because it has become inhospitable and unhomely. The only way to live with this situation, then, is to go away from time to time or to protest and rebel. The demonstrations of the young in various cities have been caused, at least partly, by the continuous shrinking of living space, which has produced a feeling of being boxed up – a feeling felt by many adults as well. Where can people develop, where can they find time and space for self-realization, where can they experiment, where can they exercise responsibility in a world where everything is already planned, regimented, ordered and prescribed? The demands for total mobility, high economic growth and the economic use of living space have limited our freedom of movement and action. And this is the reason why our towns have become ungovernable.

I I

Changing values: opportunities for a new society

The purpose of life and new ideals: leisure time – the driving force of change

Great upheavals are taking place all around us. In one or two decades the world will be a very different place. A fundamentally different society is emerging, capable of the best or of the worst. Once again we find ourselves at a beginning – this is the encouraging and at the same time disconcerting feeling among an increasing number of people. Value structures and life styles of work-oriented industrial society, accepted unquestionably for many generations, are now being criticized, the meaning of life, its goals and quality are being re-examined and redefined. A recent study conducted by the Stanford Research Institute (USA) describes these developments as the greatest intellectual revolution since the Renaissance.[23] It has caught hold of millions of people, who are explicitly or implicitly critical of the existing system of values and are ready to try out new things in order to make their lives different and better. A number of books dealing with this revolution from different angles have been published in recent years. Their titles are revealing: *After Us the Future* (H. A. Pestalozzi), *The Aquarian Conspiracy* (M. Ferguson), *Ways out of the Prosperity Trap* (various authors), *Menschenbeben* ('Manquake', R. Jungk), *Turning Point* (F. Capra), *Roads to Paradise* (A. Gorz). We should especially bear in mind the tremendous response to Michael Ende's books *Momo* and *The Neverending Story*. His projection of man's new image and consciousness obviously corresponds to the thinking of an increasing number of people.

The focal point of this great shift is certainly the changing attitude of many people to work and the economy. Since the nineteenth century our society has been increasingly shaped by economic factors. Until just a few years ago, work was still unquestionably accepted as the pivot of life by a society whose unchallenged ideals were achievement, success, recognition, property and wealth. They could be attained through efficiency, diligence, ambition, discipline, obedience, a sense of order and duty.[24] Now, at the end of the twentieth century, the original goals of the economy and of the hard-working people have actually been attained: today most people not only have the basic necessities but many other things that help to make life more pleasant. We are the generation which has, for the first time, experienced affluence. This is especially true of the young. The 'reign of necessity' has for many been replaced by the 'reign of freedom', in which intellectual and social needs play an increasingly important role. Once the basic material needs have been satisfied, it seems quite natural that our interests should shift to immaterial things. The art of living and the quality of life are increasingly placed before the standard of living. Values such as freedom, participation and self-realization are coming to the fore, while professional advancement, security and income become less important. Economic aspects and work are being demoted in the hierarchy of values. Many people are beginning to notice that more money and consumption do not necessarily bring a sense of well-being nor the opportunity to develop one's potential. People have more money and an abundance of 'goodies', but they have no time to do the things they would like to do: no time for the family, friends, for themselves, no time to be lazy. But to have time means to live.

Just as in the charming story about the little girl Momo, we no longer want our time to be stolen by some 'grey gentlemen' and invested in 'time savings banks' forever. People are rediscovering time. Money-mindedness is being replaced by time-mindedness.

The German leisure-time researcher Horst Opaschowski believes that the following elements will shape our life style in the near future:[25]

- Greater emphasis on leisure time: leisure as a medium for self-realization.
- Greater emphasis on active experience and active enjoyment of life.
- Greater emphasis on the pleasures of life.
- Greater emphasis on the present: what counts is the present, the here-and-now and not the future.
- Greater interest in nature and the environment – a back to nature where technology and progress take second place.

According to Opaschowski, it is primarily the younger generation who are now pioneering and demonstrating new life styles. He believes that they will be followed, after some time, by the middle-aged and older generations.

Be that as it may, demands for a more meaningful life, for more time to enjoy life, for life on a human scale, are now voiced not only by the few advocates of 'alternative' solutions, but they feature increasingly among the members of the 'Establishment'. More being than having – the motto coined by Erich Fromm, is attracting more and more disciples.

All the studies of changing values in our society agree about one thing: free time has become the focal point of the life style we are striving for, it is the driving force behind the change in our values.[26] Indeed, leisure time is living time par excellence. Horst Opaschowski believes that the late 1980s and 1990s will see the emergence of a 'leisure-cultural life style', which will change not only our behaviour during leisure time, but all our habits, including those at work.[27] From the 1950s to the 1970s our free time was dominated by passive consumption, typified perhaps by watching the television and drinking canned beer. The emerging 'leisure-cultural' life style as seen by Opaschowski will be oriented towards an active experience of life, with an emphasis on the following:

- Active participation instead of passive consumption; initiative, voluntary involvement.
- Self-development and spontaneity instead of organization and planning; an acceptance of the unplanned, new and unexpected experiences; imagination and creativity.
- Social contact/togetherness instead of isolation and alienation; being together with the family and friends; life in a group and the experience of belongingness.
- Relaxation/well-being instead of overwork and stress; being free from demands; being carefree and detached.
- Having a good time/enjoying life instead of being discontented and constrained; pleasure, entertainment and diversion; celebration and play.

Consumer culture or a leisure-cultural life style

The new attitude to leisure could even steer the increasing release from productive work into a positive development – less work could mean a chance for more humanism in work, leisure and life in general. There are many signs that the gentle revolution, which will reorient the value system of our industrial society is already underway and is quickly spreading. Despite these optimistic signs we should remain realistic: we are still at the beginning of a long, obstacle-ridden road and we don't know where it will end or what is awaiting us there.

First of all, we should not delude ourselves that the new life style will be everyone's choice. There will always be the ambitious careerist, the dedicated workaholic manager, the notorious consumerist; there will always be some people who are perfectly happy to live for their work, who totally identify themselves with their tasks and are literally absorbed by their occupation. Moreover, a part of our society still consists of needy and disadvantaged people, for whom the quality of life and changing values are not an issue at all, because they are still concerned with scraping together the bare necessities of life.

Furthermore, history teaches us that it always takes a long time for personal and more especially for social ideals to change. A long time is needed for the new consciousness to lead to different behaviour, for the majority to set off on a new road and for the new values to take root in the social consciousness. This development cannot be forced, it can only be supported and encouraged.

Strong resistance to the new life style springs from the general tendency to stick stubbornly to the known, the habitual. The guardians of the Holy Grail – the Established Order – are as numerous as they are influential. Public opinion and social policies are still almost unconditionally geared to growth, efficiency and work, although in their private lives many people have embraced other values and priorities. The gap between private thinking and public ideals threatens to become bigger and bigger. Despite the widespread shift in attitudes, we are still a working society and not a leisure society, a society adhering tenaciously to the traditional professional ethic and the principle of full employment in the sense of full-time employment; a society which forces us into a rigid schedule and tells us when to work, when to rest and when to go on holiday – everybody at the same time by numbers. The system goes on, although many people find it less and less acceptable and although many would be prepared to work less and earn less in order to live more.

One would expect the new life style to reverse the upward trend in consumerism: to turn a consumption-happy society into a consumption-tired one, to produce either voluntary moderation or even abstinence. But the economic system would go to war if that happened since consumption is its life blood and it will do all it can to bring the consumer up to scratch. Already in the 1960s a marketing magazine wrote that there was only one foolproof way of maintaining a continuous business boom: to raise a whole new generation of superconsumers![28] This is what many people still believe today. It goes without saying that such attitudes present a danger to these new ideals and that the individual will be put under pressure to ensure that leisure time remains essentially consumer time. If that happens Opaschowski's list will be reduced to its last element – fun and pleasure. But to lay all the blame on the hidden persuaders, i.e. the manipulating marketing of the leisure industry and speak of 'consumption terrorism', is only half the truth. After all, the system could not function without the consumers' consent – and consumers are going along with things, probably not against their own 'free' will. It is certainly a fact that the most important demands for durable consumer goods have been met in the industrialized countries. In the Federal Republic of Germany, for example, 90 per cent of all households have a telephone, 84 per cent have a car, 83 per cent a refrigerator, 80 per cent a fully automatic washing machine, 79 per cent a colour television set, 78 per cent an electric sewing machine, etc.[29] But this is still very far from what we might call the 'consumption-ceiling' – the saturation point – which is still a long way off. We have at best stilled the first hunger. As we mentioned earlier, according to sociologists and psychologists, once certain needs have been satisfied, they are immediately replaced by other desires and needs of a higher order. Either this, or the same motives simply become more ambitious. Man is obviously insatiable by nature, his needs unappeasable.[30] The current development indicates – at least for the near future – merely a shift in consumption patterns rather than a halt: money for travel around the world instead of furniture and clothes; backpacking in the tropics instead of full board in Torquay; smaller cars but more sophisticated hi-fi systems; wine instead of beer.[31] We are still a long way from a reverse in consumer behaviour trends.

Indeed, there are whole worlds between acknowledging new values and actually living by them. For example, we all claim to be aware of the need to protect the environment, but very few people are willing to take the least action themselves and reduce their own pollution of the environment. There are many ways in which this could be done: we could, for example, use public transport whenever possible instead of the car when we go to work, as well as on weekends and on holiday. We could use existing accommodation and renounce the landscape-devouring construction of weekend houses and of second and even third homes. We could enjoy nature without the need for special parking lots, or built-in facilities for sport, games, fitness and fun; we could do without funiculars, revolving restaurants and scores of other attractions. When staying at the hotel in the desert oasis we could reduce our water consumption of 600 litres per tourist per day (including the swimming pool and the sprinkled lawn), so that the natives may have enough drinking water and the date palms of the local peasants may be watered. But then, people hate to do without all these amenities when they are on holiday or relaxing. After all, this is what they have been working so hard for, isn't it? For once they just are not going to save – not even if they make life difficult for other people and certainly not on holiday!

More and more money is being spent on leisure. Leisure budgets have been rising at an explosive rate, much faster than all other expenditure. Travel and holidays come at the absolute top of the spending list. The leisure budget of the Germans, for example, more than quadrupled between 1965 and 1982.[32] Almost a third of this leisure money goes into the holidays, followed by, in order of importance, the car, the television, the radio, gardening and pets, sport and camping, games and toys, hobbies and do-it-yourself, theatre, cinema, education and entertainment, photography and film. Roughly two monthly incomes per year are currently spent on leisure activities and the upward trend in leisure consumption is expected to continue to rise in the coming years, with expenditure on other goods and services stagnating or even declining.

We live in a world of overwhelming material temptations. The leisure industry produces enormous quantities of attractive consumer goods and this glut in supply is threatening to choke and crush the recent and still hesitant desire for more purposeful and personal development. How can the door to the inner Self be found in the presence of so much superficiality? We are urged to be disciplined at work, but to pursue excess, pleasure, mobility, prestige and consumerism during our free time. The manifold supply by the leisure and entertainment industries serves the purpose of keeping the people caught by consumer-culture happy, rather than developing their abilities, which remain fallow during their working lives. Is there also a danger that continuous activity and mass movement, the wave of experiences, and the never-ceasing gregariousness and group pressure will result in leisure stress? A new and subtle form of loneliness can develop: the inner loneliness felt in the midst of a flood of contacts and hectic activity.

We all find it easier to swim with the tide, especially during the holidays. We don't always do it out of conviction, but because it is convenient, perhaps even because we do not know how to do otherwise. To reach the source, we must go against the current and that is hard, dangerous and all but comfortable. Since everyday life is rough, we do not want the holidays to be problem-ridden. So we let it be and consume what we are offered, although deep down we are longing for something else.

It will now perhaps be easier to understand why a new society, however desirable, cannot develop overnight. The development of a new understanding of leisure time and travel is an equally long process. We must therefore ask ourselves whether the new ethos for living can assert itself against the powerful established system or whether the movement will end right where it had begun its rebellion: in dependence, passive consumption, in the old, endless cycle of new demands and in fleeting moments of consumer happiness. The question is, then, whether the new, idealistic image of man will be shattered by the hard reality of the competitive materialistic society and whether the great changes on the horizon will peter out into nothing.

All my hopes rest on the young people of today. Tomorrow, they will be in power and in a position to change society. They will certainly take the struggle for a new life style a step further and perhaps even achieve a breakthrough. The omens are certainly favourable, particularly in view of:[33]

- The ability of at least some young people to assert themselves with 'cheerful sovereignty' against the laws of industrial society.
- The growing ability of many young people to live according to their own needs, as well as their refusal to be told what their priorities should be.
- Their fresh sensitivity to nature.

So, I take an optimistic view of the future; I am confident that the attempts to humanize society, which are now underway in many areas, will make progress in the long run. This applies to work and leisure time, to everyday life and travel. It is therefore worth our while to think about it.

Ways out of the work crisis

The change in people's attitude to work and their wish for a new life style are not sufficient to lead the working society out of the crisis but it is a very good starting point. Over and above that, concerted efforts will have to be made to get out of the straitjacket imposed on society by the industrial-economic system and established work policies. A few cosmetic corrections will not do the job, though. The concept of the humanization of work does not exhaust itself in the idea, for instance, that one has nothing against one's colleague putting a cage with a pet hamster on his desk. If our goal is a new form of work, i.e. work with a human face, we shall need to cut deep into the existing system and change the basic presuppositions. The humanization of work should not be merely a fashionable slogan suffering from acute anaemia. It should become the guiding principle in a series of strategies and policies designed to give us a new appreciation of, and a new approach to, work, economy and life. There are many directions in which we could divert the crisis train carrying the working society. It is time now to start laying the tracks – although a safe passage cannot be guaranteed.

Solution 1: Make work more satisfying
This humanization strategy is aimed at counteracting the loss of purpose in present-day occupational work. Based on more participation and responsibility, its measures may include: a less stringent division of labour through a wider range of tasks and more responsibility (job enrichment, job enlargement, job rotation); more participation in decision making; more independence and co-operation, for example in the form of partly autonomous working groups, more training and education programmes, both on and off the job; greater emphasis on human and social relationships in the firm and on the social usefulness of the job. This strategy, we should point out, can only help those already at work. It would have no influence with the redundant or unemployed.

Solution 2: A new distribution of work
Unemployment is the most inhumane, absurd and certainly the most expensive form of shorter working hours. This time-bomb can be defused only if the available work is divided among more heads and hands. The postulate 'work less so that everyone may work' is of paramount importance to the future for humanitarian, social and economic reasons. It is absurd to have a situation in which a declining number of people work until exhaustion, while an increasing number of other people are condemned to idleness. There are various possibilities for shorter working hours: a shorter working day (e.g. a seven-hour day), a shorter working week (e.g. a thirty-five-hour week,

a limit on overtime, a four-day week), a shorter working year (e.g. longer holidays), a shorter working life (e.g. a sabbatical year, earlier retirement). If the latest surveys are to be believed, already today as many as 35 per cent of German and 47 per cent of Swiss employees would be prepared to work less and earn less.[34] A scheme utilizing this potential of volunteers would help to reduce unemployment to some extent, but it would not solve the problem. A generally binding reduction of working hours is unavoidable if unemployment is to be brought under control. Incomes will also have to be curtailed in the process. But these reductions will be small, because higher productivity can be achieved even with less work. It is advisable to distribute the gains made by these measures in the form of shorter working time and not as higher wages. Those who are really serious about reducing current and future unemployment, will have to adopt this course of action. But the new allocation of work will bring about real humanization only if the rigid working time schedule, and especially the tripartite division 'education – work – retirement' in the course of a lifetime is abandoned. The lowering of the retirement age is by no means the only or the best possibility for working less. The new allocation of work must therefore go hand in hand with more flexible time schedules.

Solution 3: The new, flexible time schedule
This principle, also called 'time sovereignty', envisages a more flexible planning of life: people are offered a wide range of possibilities for using their time. They can decide themselves when and how much they want to work and how much money they want to earn. There are countless variations on the theme of more flexible time schedules. For example:[35]

- A thirty-five-hour week 'à la carte'; e.g. 5 times 7, or 4 times 8.75 working hours per day; or more days off, or longer holidays after several years.
- More flexible daily working hours.
- More part-time jobs.
- Half-yearly choice of the working week: e.g. a thirty-hour week in the summer and a forty-hour week in the winter.
- Annual working time contracts: e.g. a total of 1500 working hours per annum with a monthly minimum of 100 hours.
- Introduction of new working cycles; e.g. ten days on ten days off, or work from Monday until Thursday and then from Tuesday until Saturday.

- Job-sharing; e.g. two co-workers share the job and working hours to their convenience.
- Sabbaticals; e.g. every employee has the right to take a longer period off once every ten years without losing his job.
- Work even at an older age; e.g. after the age of fifty-five every employee can decide him or herself when to retire or gradually reduce the amount of work he or she does.

A more flexible working time, then, would solve many work-related problems. It would satisfy many people's desire for more 'living' time, help solve problematic situations at work, make possible a staggered entry into and exit from the job, reduce the gap between work and leisure time and help in solving many mass-related problems produced by simultaneous working hours. Were we to devote only a part of the time and imagination employed in achieving technological progress to a rethinking of outdated working-time schedules, the results could be spectacular. What is needed is less technological and more social imagination. A number of eminent thinkers believe that by the end of this century we shall need less than half the working hours currently spent on the maintenance of our living standard. They suggest, for example, that people should be given an obligatory minimum of working hours per lifetime, which could be used in a flexible way and for which they would be awarded a minimum 'citizen's wage'. Everybody would be free to work in addition to that, earning the corresponding wage, or decide to do without additional material blessings and pursue their hobbies and other interests.[36] The philosopher Bertrand Russell has long since been joined by many other like-minded people in his Utopia for a better life. It was several decades ago that Russell wrote the following: 'And with modern technique it would be possible to distribute leisure justly without injury to civilisation. I mean that four hours' work a day should entitle a man to the necessities and elementary comforts of life, and that the rest of his time should be his to use as he might see fit. It is an essential part of any such social system that education should be carried further than it usually is at present, and should aim, in part, at providing tastes which would enable a man to use leisure intelligently.'[37]

Solution 4: The new dual economy
This most comprehensive of all humanization strategies presupposes a fundamental reorientation of our economic system and must be interpreted as a positive Utopia for a distant future. The dual economy

alternative is based on a bipartite economic system, in which both parts complement each other. On one side is the formal industrial market economy, whose growth, however, is strictly controlled and channelled in qualitative terms. This sector should employ as many people as possible working significantly shorter hours and producing socially useful and necessary goods. Monetary economic expansionism, the continuous growth of production and the trend to a total marketization and 'economization' will be brought to a halt. They will be replaced by quality-oriented economic policies, with a number of new or re-evaluated areas of work, for example the reorganization of cities and their agglomerations, the development of specific services such as health education, outpatient medical care, vocational education, an increase in leisure-related activities in the social, cultural and educational fields.

On the other side is the informal private or domestic economic sector, in which individual work and self-help in the local community must be revived and re-evaluated for example by making available land and buildings, workshop equipment and setting up the necessary educational programmes. Many activities which were taken 'out of the house' with advancing industrial development must be brought 'back home', at least in part. Thus, for example, private businesses and self-help organizations run by private households or local communities could be set up, using perhaps 'domestic type' electronic information and communication systems. The kinds of community activity could range from vegetable growing and handicrafts, to medical self-help, the care of the sick and elderly, education and training, neighbourhood guidance and counselling, etc.[38] Although such a dual economy would undoubtedly produce a certain reduction in incomes, the diminished amount of work and money from the formal sector could certainly be partly compensated by more work in the informal sector. Moreover, the loss would probably be more than made up for by a gain in the quality of life, the feeling of satisfaction and purpose, as well as by individual freedom and social responsibility. On the whole, people would probably work more, but their activity would be 'individual', in other words, they would not have freedom from work but freedom at work. Finally, the smaller economic and social networks would be a favourable precondition for providing checks on the explosion of government centralization and expenditure. The dual alternative is the human form of economy and life for the after-tomorrow.

The restoration of homeliness

Homeliness is not something objective or measurable, it cannot be expressed in the number of bedrooms, in the size of the garden or in the number of sports and leisure facilities. It is an entirely subjective feeling. A town, a neighbourhood, a street, a house or a flat are homely if they provide the opportunity for self-development, for contacts with other people, for expressing one's own personality, and creativity. Homeliness is above all the result of participation: when the inhabitants can make their own contribution and change their own environment. It is people who create homeliness. But the homeliness of the past cannot simply be brought back to our modern cities. It is as impossible as turning back the clock. It is impossible to make good the colossal blunders that have been made in more recent town planning. But painstaking work on detail can succeed in stopping the further desolation of towns and neighbourhoods and restore a part of the lost living space. This movement, which in recent years has been gaining support in many towns, is not just a passing fad, a wave of nostalgia, it expresses the people's need for harmony and warmth, it is a reaction against alienation. More and more people are taking the initiative, setting up neighbourhood groups and action committees in order to make their homes and neighbourhoods 'cosier', more snug. A new neighbourhood awareness is emerging. Municipal authorities, planners and architects are also changing their approach. Traffic control, integrated architecture, structural buildings, are the new catch phrases in the technical jargon. These principles should create better preconditions for more homeliness – which is badly needed. But our environment can become homely only when the vast mass of the people themselves become actively involved. There are hundreds of ways how this can happen. Many possibilities have already been tested and have proved to be feasible. Everybody can participate and those who are interested can consult various brochures, reports, leaflets and other publications containing instructions and advice. Here are some of them: *The Handbook for Neighbourhood Improvers (Handbuch für Quartier-Verbesserer,* Zürich 1980),[39] Free Space – Tolerance Space' *(Freiräume – Toleranzräume)* published by the Zürich Working Group for Town Planning (Zürich 1981),[40] the handbook *Free Time in Lucerne (Freizeit in Luzern,* Luzern 1981).[41] The following ideas and suggestions come largely from these three reports. First of all a few general demands which illustrate the 'philosophy' put forward by their authors.

The sensual city
'The natural relationship with the basic elements water, soil, rocks, plants, wood and fire must be learned again. Where are the small streams that can be damned? Where is the place for a camp fire? Where can a child experience how to build a small wooden hut?' '. . . Where can people experience a natural, direct contact with animals? Where is the rabbit house, the small poultry yard?'

The unfinished city
'We must create new open areas, zones where something that is not lucrative can take place. Areas which are not totally organized.' . . . 'What we need are numerous niches . . . areas which are unfinished and provide room for creativity, for a – limited – creative disorder, for inhabitants' actions. Hollows should be left in new constructions for children to build in their own quarters . . .' Leave room for an 'architectural smile'. Not too much perfection. Not too much regimentation.

The living city
'Life in a city means density, mixing, diversity, coexistence and not separation or division. Any restriction of the diverse possibilities of existence encourages one-sidedness and the prevalence of a single function' . . . 'We want no sterile division of functions. What we want is coexistence and togetherness . . .'

The communicative city
'We must never stop trying to create contact.'

The human city:
'What we lack is tolerance; the acceptance of the fact that our fellow-citizens are different, that there are different needs – those of children, the young, the elderly, of mothers, foreigners, workers, intellectuals . . . We all too often expect others to do something instead of starting at our own door. A city can become more human only if the people are human.'

What can be done in the flat, the house or in the neighbourhood? For example:

● Give the tenant more freedom and responsibility. Give him the chance to shape his own environment. Promote a certain degree of tenants' self-management.

- Living together: Give the caretaker less responsibility and the tenants more. Hold tenants' meetings and discuss problems relating to the flats and the building. Joint adoption of house rules. Task sharing. Promote housing co-operatives and associations.
- Renovation instead of demolition. All buildings should, if possible, be regularly maintained and not pulled down. Gentle renovation, i.e. repair and improvement of what is most necessary on a continuous basis. No luxury renovations. Self-initiative and participation of tenants in the planning and renovation work.
- Reconvert former housing space – notably all offices – into flats.
- Promote multi-purpose construction (for housing, work, play, recreation) and social mixing (the elderly and the young, families and single persons).
- Expand the amount of open and green areas and playgrounds for children per housing unit.
- When designing new blocks of flats or housing developments, plan communal rooms for the inhabitants, workshops or hobby rooms, and rooms for children to play in.
- Coloured and original façades, designed by tenants, on blocks of flats.
- Promote flat ownership on a broad basis.
- Promote the construction of compact and structured housing estates instead of family houses occupying wide areas.

Many of these proposals are addressed above all to the real estate policies of public authorities. But there are also enlightened private owners, landlords, contractors and architects as well as enterprising tenants, who can do a lot of things.

What can be done in the neighbourhood? For example:

- Provide play areas for children instead of the prefabricated playgrounds with concrete pipes, sand boxes and slides, e.g. areas between houses where children can play soccer, build huts and caves.
- Provide allotment gardens: large unused grass plots can be fenced off and divided into allotments. Interested tenants have the possibility of leasing an allotment and planting vegetables and flowers.
- Natural gardens instead of the ubiquitous grass plots; leave some open areas, where nature is given the chance to develop on its own.
- Preserve and expand existing allotments in the neighbourhood and in the greater town area. Abandon the requirement for standardized garden sheds.
- Make asphalted front yards green again.

- Improve and revitalize back yards and transform them into meeting places.
- Give the streets back to the people: 'Residential streets are snail's pace streets, quiet streets, streets on which everything is possible, streets for strollers.'
- Squares for everyone. Squares should be used for various purposes. Remove obstacles and prohibition signs which limit availability. Allow diverse happenings and uses: markets, street cafés, theatres, concerts, provision for notice boards and newsletters, 'Hyde Park Corners'.
- Treat local pubs as buildings worthy of preservation.
- Open schools to the public for sports or entertainment events, for gourmets' groups, workshops, etc.
- Provide meeting places for the young. Every neighbourhood should have a youth club.
- Set up neighbourhood clubs and organize neighbourhood entertainment.

What can be done in the greater city area and in transport? For example:

- Decentralize sports and leisure facilities wherever possible and make them accessible to everyone. Fight the ghettoization of sports and cultural institutions, the one-sided use of facilities and oversized centres.
- Popularize the big cultural institutions and events, often described as elitist, above all the theatre, museums and concerts; take them to various parts of town.
- Limit private car transport and promote public transport; the two measures must go hand in hand. A reduction in individual transport can be achieved through the introduction of speed limits, car-free zones, pedestrian zones, streets closed to car traffic with feeder service, restrictive parking policies with preferential treatment for residents, smaller and more strictly controlled parking areas, development of the park-and-ride system, financial measures including higher taxes, the construction of underground garages and parking lots. In promoting public transport the following measures should be considered; attractively designed vehicles, the expansion of the public transport network both in the city and in the agglomerations, improved schedules and tariff measures including free transport. And last but by no means least: promote bicycle transport by building special lanes. Similar transport and traffic policies should be adopted for recreational travel, in the town environs and for holiday

resorts, where problems are very similar to those encountered in cities.

There are many roads to a homelier city. If something is done on all these levels, it is not unrealistic to hope that gradually new qualities will be added to life at home. This development will be enhanced by changing values and priorities; where free time is the focal point of life, the home will become increasingly important. Should working hours be further reduced and the domestic economy and work at home revived and encouraged, then we will again become real 'settlers' or at least have a closer relationship to the home. It is to be hoped, then, that the numbers of neighbourhood and city improvers will be much larger tomorrow than they are today: more people will be ready to come out of the isolation of their residential quarters, get together with others and do something for the restoration of homeliness. There will also be more politicians, planners, architects, contractors, landlords and proprietors, cultural, church and other institutions who will also understand the issues and themselves become active.

What can he be thinking about? Perhaps that his village has become a 'resort' and his country a playground and that he is in fact sorry about it.

For all those who haven't noticed yet: tourism is supposed to be business, not charity.

Tourism creates two categories of people: those who serve and those who are served. This may lead to feelings of inferiority and superiority.

Their only contacts are 'handouts' – how can this lead to meaningful communication? Tourists as the new maharajahs.

Several thousand tourists visit his hut during the season. Can we blame this herdsman for not being exactly overjoyed at the arrival of each new group?

Tourist development determined by strangers. People from the city have the money, they buy up the land, they develop and build. They control many things. But they don't live here, or only occasionally. The anonymous 'letter box people'.

'The Third World is the brothel of industrialized countries' (F. Fanon). Sex travel is the most inhuman form of tourism, the worst exploitation and humiliation. But it's roaring business. Some tour operators act as pimps. And they go unpunished.

Was everything only an illusion? A holiday theatre? Three weeks of sparkle and glitter? And then the curtain — the lights go out. Over — till next time?

Or does something remain? Travelling as exploration and a learning ground – as a 'school of life'?

Isn't there growing evidence that a new travel culture is emerging, that tourists are becoming more emancipated and that they are tactfully 'adopting' the foreign environment?

Or are travel memories only souvenirs which people collect like stamps and put on the mantelpiece like some kind of trophy?

The natives are getting ready for rebellion. They are still doing (almost) everything to attract tourists, but what they would really like to do is prevent them from coming.

The desolate home environment . . .

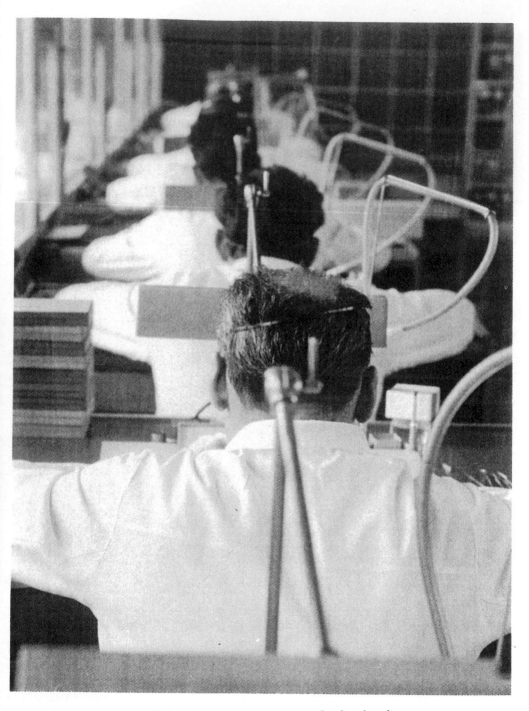

. . . the seemingly hopeless situation in a standardized and oppressive work environment,

. . . and the barren and artificial urban environment,

. . . are the reasons why people long to escape from everyday life.
Their desires have emigrated to a dream world and they would love
to follow them.

But the 'greatest intellectual revolution since the Renaissance' has broken out: the new life-style-movement with leisure as its focal point. Its driving force is principally the young, on whom all our hopes must be pinned. They may accomplish what we haven't been able to do: the humanization of everyday life.

It is never too late for social fantasy — the future is what we make it.

Only if we succeed in living with tourism as a mass phenomenon, and develop forms of individualization and humanization from that position, can we make a step forward.

'Sheep instead of tourists' – the development of a tourism which obliterates all other economic activities must be prevented in the interest of both locals and tourists themselves.

For the locals, balanced tourist development means, above all, locally controlled use of land and carefully planned step-by-step development. Otherwise it will follow that familiar pattern: from a seemingly harmless beginning . . .

. . . to the all-engulfing and irreversible tourist colonization.

Relaxed self-confidence and a consistent commitment to one's own culture are the most effective weapons against 'touristification'. The tourist should adapt to the country and the people he is visiting – not the other way round. Local flowers instead of imported whisky.

Holidays toward the Self. Discovering one's own abilities – looking at things with different eyes.

Use the holidays for self-discovery. Share happiness. Be there for others. Have time for them. Do not look always for the exotic, the extreme – enjoy the little holiday pleasures.

Be a considerate traveller: 'look' instead of 'look down on' – ask instead of answer – search instead of find.

Animation should be interpreted as unobtrusive guidance to more meaningful leisure and travel. The untrained, inhibited and uncommunicative 'everyday man' needs encouragement and stimuli to become aware of the many leisure opportunities.

'Travel is life — in the same way as life is a journey' (Jean Paul). Take to the road together. Include the excluded.

Preparation for travel from childhood. Solidarity instead of egoism, togetherness instead of isolation. Going towards instead of going away. Tourism instigating a more humane society? Yes, why not?

PART FOUR

Proposals for the Humanization of Travel

How can we get from extensive to intensive
    travel,
from devouring miles to lingering,
from ticking off items in the travel guide to
    stopping and thinking,
from rush to leisure,
from aggressive and destructive to creative com-
    munication,
from camera-wearing idiots to people with the
    third eye?
I believe
these are the important and burning issues.
For we are all looking for meaning and humanity.

Al Imfeld

12

The strategies and their philosophies

Create a new, better tourism – what a utopian undertaking! How can this enormous machinery be changed? We said at the very beginning of our book what our general principles and ideas should be and what we should be striving for: 'The ideal we need is a harmonized co-operative world in which each part is a centre, living at the expense of nobody else, in partnership with nature in solidarity with future generations.'[1] Having analysed how the holiday machinery works, we can now see even more clearly how apt this formulation is. Humanization refers to all the measures which bring us closer to that situation, be it in the area of travel or any other field.

Before presenting our thoughts about the proposals for better travel and a desirable future, let us emphasize once again that in itself, a new tourist awareness can produce few, if any, practical results if it is not embedded in a new life style,[2] to travel but encompasses all aspects of our existence. What we need in the first place are not different ways of travelling but different people. Only a new society and a new everyday situation can produce a new tourist. A sick society cannot produce healthy tourists. Everyday life must change if travel is to change. It is therefore pointless to chase the phantom of 'genuine' travel and imagine that people can be taught how to pursue such a myth.[3] What we must understand is the relationship and interaction between work, home, leisure and travel. Man is an indivisible social being, and cannot be neatly parcelled up into working man, leisure man, weekend man and holiday man. What he needs is self-realization and fulfilment in all spheres of life. There is no escape from oneself, not even on holiday. As has already been pointed out, the everyday situation shapes the traveller, in the same way as travel experiences can influence everyday life. Does that mean we shall have better tourism only when the society from which it springs becomes better itself? Or should we nevertheless make a start in the world of travel and improve some of its aspects? This may itself produce some desires for a better life in general and take us a step further in the search for a more humanistic society. It is a chance that shouldn't be allowed to slip through our fingers.

Below, I present my ideas about the humanization of travel in the form of a number of proposals which should be read as a rough draft or sketch of an attitude and as possible guidelines rather than a binding and definitive system. I do not make a scientific claim with it, but submit it to the reader as an expression of my personal conviction and hope. Their breakdown into twenty-three headings is arbitrary and should facilitate reference. The same goes for the titles and the use of italics. Of course, the greatest effect would be achieved by implementing not just one or two but a combination of all the proposed measures. But a start can be made anywhere. The important thing is to make one – no matter where.

Advocate a soft and humane tourism – re-evaluate the ultimate goals

I do not belong to those critics of tourism who, due to its negative consequences, would like to limit it drastically, or even abolish it altogether, though I do have some understanding for such severe reactions. Tourism can sometimes be devastating, inhuman and self-destructive. I must admit that as a scientist I am often tempted to see my duty in the prevention of tourism rather than in its improvement. I cannot observe the worldwide effects of tourism without great concern, nor can I help being disappointed at the lack of positive action aimed at improving the current state of affairs despite many useful proposals. But it is simply not true that the only alternative to present-day tourism is no tourism at all. There are other possibilities. For many people – not least for both tourists and their hosts – tourism is of vital importance and we must therefore pursue a positive goal and defend travel. But we can do it with a clear conscience only if tourism changes, if it improves. Our analysis has shown very clearly: things cannot go on in this way. Those who live as tourists and those who live off tourists must become aware of the fact and accept a new hierarchy of values. *Their common goal must be to develop and promote new forms of tourism, which will bring the greatest possible benefit to all the participants – travellers, the host population and the tourist business, without causing intolerable ecological and social damage.* We have so far neither sought nor found such forms, nor mentioned how they would be implemented.

The *main objective of a humane and environment-oriented tourist policy* may also be formulated as follows:

To guarantee the optimum satisfaction of the manifold tourist needs for people of all classes within the framework of efficient structures and in an undamaged environment, while taking into consideration the interests of the local population.[4]

This means: policies for tourism will no longer be guided only by economic and technological considerations, but will also take into account environment conservation and the needs of all those involved in tourism. Tourism which meets these conditions I propose to call '*soft tourism*' or 'adapted tourism' (after the arguments in favour of an adapted technology); tourism, on the other hand, whose policies are dictated only by economic and technological factors may be called 'hard tourism'. Nobody will deny the fact that the latter has prevailed so far, everywhere and without exception.

The precondition for a reorientation from hard to soft tourism is an unambiguous acknowledgement of the new priorities: the focal point of everything must be people. It is important to realize that tourism has been created for people and not the other way round. The purpose of all development, then, including tourist development, should be to develop man and not things. Human development should be the primary aim: human virtues, social abilities, and a moral world view the guiding principles. We are not talking here about an 'ideal superman' but a 'new' man, in which the new can be created from the old. Tourism, then, must be given back to man and thus made more human.

These demands are by no means new. They have been made for some time now by various people, especially scientists. But the wire-pullers have not taken them up so far. The resolutions, recommendations, postulates and studies that have been published by many institutions and authors in recent years all make the same call for a new orientation in tourist policies. However, the policy-makers have so far ignored these calls. The 'thinkers' who sit in their studies are political lightweights. Their recommendations will remain politically anaemic theories as long as there is no pressure on the politicians from the general public – both tourists and their hosts. Only when people refuse to accept and to co-operate, will practical policies and the reality change. What we need, then, are rebellious tourists and rebellious locals. There are developments in this area which give us more than a glimmer of hope. We have already commented on them extensively. There is the general change in social values and the trend towards more humanity in everyday life, which holds a promise for the humanization of travel as well. With this in the background, the process of the emancipation of tourists will make further progress: the manipulated tourists will be gradually replaced by increasingly informed, critical and mature tourists, people who respond, react and participate. And finally, the changing attitudes in the population of the tourist destination areas are an important new force. There is a growing awareness of the problems that tourism creates, a growing self-confidence and a stronger will for self-determined development.

I believe, then, that in the foreseeable future there is a real chance for essential changes in tourist policies. The situation is open, the awareness of problems high as never before. We must therefore press home our point and insist more than ever on the need for man-oriented policies in tourism. Should policy-makers continue to centre on growth and the narrow interests of the tourist trade, sooner or later they will be faced with rebellion, one by tourists and one by the locals – against tourists.[5]

Take steps in the right direction without waiting for the great change

The possibility of a turning point towards a better tourism is in sight. However, it is still uncertain whether the breakthrough will succeed. *It is important to help as many as possible of the people involved to a new critical awareness*, because it is only then, when they are aware of their condition, that they may perhaps change their behaviour. This is the hardest step of all but it is the crucial one.

We want to continue on this road. This is why we shall not paint a picture of an ideal, but unreachable (travel-)society. This Utopia will never exist, for its adversaries are too powerful. How can we overcome the almighty business-is-business principle or the unbridgeable North-South gap? What we need are not solely long-term goals, objectives that can be reached only in a very distant future. If that were the case we could only wait and hope. The future can be what we make of it and not what we let happen. We therefore need short-term goals – things that can be tackled here and now in order to anticipate on a small scale part of the future. Our proposals for the humanization of travel cannot and will not be all-conclusive, but will rather be an outline of the *general direction to be followed*. If we really want to change the travel system, we should keep in mind what is feasible: thus we are not proposing the dismantling of the system but its slow transformation undertaken step by step.

The appropriate conditions for the gentle revolution must be created through small steps, each one leading to a new awareness, which itself helps us to take the next step.

The question already discussed about whether we should first try to change society or ourselves resembles the dilemma about the chicken and the egg. We must do both at the same time, i.e. adopt a double strategy. If one should take place without the other, it would be much less effective and even end in failure. Where individual people are not aware of the need for change and are not ready to contribute to it, new legislation will produce no effect. On the other hand, changes in specific areas can only be fully effective if they are supported by new social regulations which everybody must observe. *Changes can and must get underway everywhere. They need not always be spectacular reforms. Indeed, it is the 'small personal revolution' that can have equal importance in improving travel.* After all, every individual tourist builds up or destroys human values while travelling. Viewed in this light, even the smallest step in the right direction is significant; the individual must become active and take the initiative without waiting for others, regardless of what the scale of his action is. The slogan must be: *global thinking – local action.* We must try to do it differently for once – beginning with the simple things right at our front doors. The adventure is just round the corner! We need to experiment and see what happens when we change some of our habits. It is only through *first-hand experience* that we can find out whether something new and different is better for us. But: *the new must produce a gain and not a loss for the participating individual.* It must make his life more fulfilling and enjoyable. The proposals must therefore be as 'infectious' as possible. Orders and prohibitions will not do the job – because it is not a bad conscience that we need to make progress but positive experience, not the feeling of compulsion but that of responsibility.

Provide the right interpretation of freedom in leisure and tourism policies

For many people the holidays are the last bastion of freedom. *Tourism policies, must be based, as far as possible, on the principle of voluntariness and absence of constraint; they must ensure the possibility of self-determination for all participants.* If we want the idea of leisure to stand for that which it in fact is, i.e. free time, we must prevent all attempts to usurp it for commercial gain or any other purpose.[6] Guidelines for improving the quality of travel must not degenerate into rules for regimentation and manipulation. They must make the experience of freedom possible. Leisure policy must under no circumstances be used as a disguise for attempts to impose an even subtler form of manipulation. This raises the question: should leisure and travel be totally private matters, an unlimited free area where any kind of behaviour is permitted? Certainly not! is the answer, because the free space of one person borders on that of another. Furthermore, the costs and benefits of travel are distributed unevenly, we will still have the privileged and the disadvantaged; and, finally, because besides the short-term interests of the individual there are long-term collective interests of society; the imposition of certain rules, therefore, seems desirable and necessary. Tourism is no exception to the general rule that people seldom do voluntarily that which in the long run turns out to be in the common interest. The free market does not behave better in tourism than anywhere else: it has not solved problems of growth, wasteful exploitation, destruction of the environment and the exploitation of the weak, nor has it alleviated the appalling difference between the starving poor and the feasting rich or taken into account the interests of future generations.[7] To believe in self-regulating mechanisms would be naive and dangerous. Without certain restrictions imposed above all by the state, a totally unrestrained and free leisure time and travel would lead to anarchy and chaos. *Leisure and tourist policies – yes! Not in order to introduce ideological models of society in the relatively control-free area of leisure, but to prevent unrestrained self-development from impinging on the life of others and exploiting the environment. In other words, limits must be set and conditions formulated so that leisure and travel lead to more consideration for other people.* More togetherness instead of isolation, more solidarity instead of egoism, more co-operation instead of competition. The message is clear: not less but more free space for everybody – for ourselves, for those we visit, for our children who come after us – this is the freedom I am writing about.

Accept the mass character of travel and one's own role as tourist

All proposals for the humanization of travel must take into account a very important factor, which many critics and reformers choose to ignore; namely, the quite legitimate simple wishes of the average tourist. It is precisely these wishes that we should consider before anything else, certainly before the needs of a small elite. Very many tourists simply want to recuperate – and they need rest because they are exhausted from a year of work. They also want to relax, to get temporarily away from the depressing routine and experience a kind of 'counter-world'. For example, it is perfectly normal and reasonable that many people should choose the passive enjoyment of luxury in a ghetto-like hotel and refuse to think about political and social problems for a while. Under modern conditions of life, the whole purpose and attraction of holidays for many people lies in the fact that for a while, they need not do anything 'useful'. Holidays as 'non-sense.'[8] No proposals for more 'meaningful' travel for the masses can be offered without consideration of these elementary facts. The needs and desires of the average tourist must not be excluded from the measures taken to improve tourism. On the contrary: *only if we succeed in living with tourism as a mass phenomenon, and develop forms of individualization and humanization from that position, can we claim to have made a decisive step forward.* Some forms of more meaningful travel will certainly first be embraced by a critical minority, for instance, by the relatively few people who are prepared to put up with the 'stress of enlightened conscious travel'.[9] But such minorities have always been the forerunners of positive change and development on a more massive basis.

Many of us – travellers and exponents of the tourist trade – have a distorted attitude to travel as a mass phenomenon and to our own individual tourist role. It is therefore important to underline that efforts to improve travel must be based on two realizations. These have been very aptly formulated by Hans Prahl and Albrecht Steinecke in their remarkable book *The Million Holiday.* The first is: *we must finally accept the mass character of tourism.* The contradictions inherent in mass tourism can be eliminated only by getting involved in it – on a different practical and conscious level – and not by trying to escape from it.[10] We must therefore halt the feverish competition, in which new destinations are being discovered, activities contrived, new forms of holidays and rarities offered, all for the sake of a would-be 'individual tourism' and of an imaginary obligation to be 'original' at any price.

The second realization, which is in fact a corollary of the first one and is essential for more conscious travel behaviour is *a realistic evaluation of one's own tourist role.*[11] No matter how reluctant we are to accept it, no matter how hard we try to run away from other tourists and are tempted to disguise ourselves in order not to be recognized as tourists, even if we imagine we are more locals than tourists . . . we are and remain tourists. And, for that matter, not a priori better tourists than other people. Once we have accepted this simple fact we have laid the cornerstone for more openness, tolerance, modesty and communication in travel. 'I'm OK – you're OK.'

Organize a better distribution of tourist flows

Many, though certainly not all the problems produced by modern travel, can be explained by two well-known phenomena: the tremendous concentration of holidays and travel into just a few weeks and weekends, and the congestion it produces: everybody at the same time, for the same reason, in the same places. The flight from the mass into the mass. The concentration of holidays in time and space is responsible for the huge plague of travellers, who are sometimes perceived as a burden and a threat both by tourists themselves and their hosts. The over-exploitation of recreational areas can be explained by these reasons too. Despite that, it is debatable whether many travellers would want to be quite alone on their trip. Even if they did, moving so many thousands of people, all at the same time, to their holiday homes and back again, can never be done in smaller units. So it looks as though massivity is here to stay. What we should try to do is control and reduce its scale. The question of tolerable numbers must be a central issue for the planning of tourism in the tourist destination areas. Misquoting Paracelsus, we might say that administered in small doses, tourism can be a medicine, but too much of it can act as poison. As long as the tourist waves smash on to the holiday areas, the question of psychological and ecological carrying capacity will remain unresolved. Tourist destination areas and the people who live there are simply overrun by tourists and the flood gates, if they exist at all, are swept away.

• *Efforts must therefore be made to break down the travel periods by staggering school and works holidays. Information about the advantages of staggered holidays should be made available at all levels. This question must be given a new priority in international organizations (e.g. the World Tourism Organization, the OECD, the EEC, etc.) and take its place in national policies as well.*

• *Tourist facilities in holiday areas should be more rationally distributed following the principle of 'decentralized concentration'. The tourist infrastructure should be expanded to a larger number of centres and small-scale projects should be promoted so that less developed areas get a share of the economic benefit produced by tourism.*

That the holiday period should be staggered as a matter of urgency is now generally accepted. But there is also widespread resignation about the fact that decades of political discussions about the subject have produced no tangible results. People seem to have resigned themselves to the holiday rush, accepting it as an immutable fact of life. But renewed efforts to change this situation must be made, for their success would significantly improve the preconditions for the well-being of all participants in tourism and for the preservation of recreational areas. If people were given more say in the organization and scheduling of their working and leisure time, every person would have a much greater possibility of avoiding the holiday peaks and bottlenecks; whether he or she would use the chance is less certain.

The second demand, namely that tourism should be decentralized and its scale thus reduced, is not so uncontroversial. The honey pot theory, as it is called, has many advocates: the best solution, they claim, is to set up large 'honey pots' – i.e. holiday centres, in which tourists will assemble in their thousands like insects looking for food, while all other areas will be kept free of the 'tourist plague'. Though other formulations are not always so extreme, growing resistance to tourist development which is engulfing the whole country, can be observed in many areas.

According to this view, tourism should be allotted certain zones and the rest of the country protected from it (see the proposition relating to artificial holiday centres). We should point out that our own demand for more decentralization does not imply that the overconcentration would be replaced by dispersion. Such a development would have dubious consequences both for the environment and society. What is needed is a middle-of-the-road solution in which the costs and benefits will be better distributed from the point of view of all participants.

Create preconditions for a fair exchange and for equal partnership

As has been amply demonstrated, tourism is, in the first place, a business, and is based on the same laws and principles as any other industry. The more its participants are aware of the fact, the better. It is equally clear that the business relations between travellers and their hosts, between the tourist generating and receiving countries are not always correct. Costs and benefits are often unequally distributed, the host population usually ending up with a bad bargain. *If we want to have a more human tourism, we must first ensure that it is based on fair economic transaction, in which the advantages and disadvantages are equally distributed between both parties.* 'Les bons comptes font des bons amis'. Which, freely translated can be taken as: 'it is only when the accounts have been settled that friendship can begin'. A number of our proposals are aimed at improving these trade relations. *The ideal for which we should be striving is a joint tackling of the problems arising from tourism, a partnership in which promoters and investors meet together with representatives of the host areas to discuss the planning and financing of tourist developments, in calculating costs and prices, organizing publicity and sales and deciding about the division of profit. What we are looking for are models of co-operation based on mutuality, equality and solidarity.*

To my knowledge there are very few examples of such co-operation. Pierre Lainé has launched four holiday resorts in France and Senegal which were planned according to the principle of 'harmonious development'.[12] These principles will be discussed later. But in the wider world realities of the tourist trade such co-operation between the metropolis and the rest, between town and country is non-existent. One-sided deals are still the rule. Investors in tourism still pursue tough, attacking marketing strategies for promoting the trade – not to mention their own interests – while host areas increasingly develop defensive strategies. For example, Third World tourist countries have been advised to group together to form their own travel agencies in order to negotiate on more equal terms with the big tour operators and compete with them. Just like the Organization of Petroleum Exporting Countries (OPEC), Third World countries could protect their interests by forming an 'Association of Eternal Sunshine Countries'.[13] An alliance of sunshine countries as a counterbalance to the big travel trusts. Wouldn't a joint effort to find solutions be more productive? Perhaps the disadvantaged areas have no other choice but to take the counteroffensive in order to get a discussion going and steer tourist development in a different direction.

13

About the concept of a balanced tourist development

Don't consider the promotion of tourism an end in itself nor a panacea – strive for a diversified economic structure – avoid a 'single-crop' economy

This proposal refers to an aspect of development which is almost never discussed in tourist target areas: that more tourism, i.e. more arrivals, more restaurants, more souvenir shops, more beds, more transport capacity, and more foreign exchange earnings – whatever the yardsticks used for measuring growth, they do not automatically mean greater well-being. Development and progress should be measured in terms of higher incomes, more satisfying jobs, social and cultural facilities, better housing, etc. The aim should not be just a higher gross national product but more gross national happiness, so to speak. The promotion and growth of tourism must never be an end in itself. But thinking and arguing in terms of growth rates and the glorification of statistical records are still widespread in tourist policy, especially now when most countries are grappling with the economic squeeze.

Nor does tourism mean a priori more success in revitalizing the economy and greater prosperity than any other economic activity, e.g. agriculture, or the manufacturing industries. But in this respect too, it is still acclaimed in many quarters as the sheet anchor, the big chance and panacea. Its inherent risks, such as strong dependence on foreign customers, seasonal ups and downs and the state of the economy are seldom mentioned. Development policies should therefore pay special attention to the following considerations:

- *Tourism should be promoted only in so far as it brings the host population the desired economic benefits, above all in the form of incomes and jobs, where this benefit is of a durable nature and does not have an adverse effect on the other qualities of life. A detailed report about the effects of the project (a cost/benefit analysis, including the economic, social and environmental effects) must be submitted before its implementation.*

● *A maximally diversified economic structure must be strived for in the tourist destination areas. Farming and forestry, handicrafts, small-scale industry and non-tourist services must be promoted and be given at least the same priority as tourist development. In areas with high tourist growth (the major tourist areas) other economic branches must be given preferential treatment.*

Under no circumstances should a development relying solely on tourism be allowed. Overreliance on any single economic activity is dangerous and in the case of the tourist trade, the risk is even greater. But this is exactly what has been happening in some popular tourist destination areas, for example in the Alpine area. In such cases regional planning and the control of the building market should be used to check the galloping growth of the tourist infrastructure and perhaps even to stop it altogether for a period. On the other hand, all available means and ingenuity must be resorted to if we are to preserve the jobs remaining outside tourism.

Here is a list of *measures* that could be adopted (they are taken from a catalogue of demands aimed at the reform of Swiss holiday areas):[14]

● The tourism-oriented construction industry must be gradually cut down and the redundant work force employed in the hotel industry (maintenance, renovation), farming and forestry, housing reconstruction and the power industry.
● A combination of compatible trades should be promoted (e.g. tourism/farming through holidays on the farm).
● Activities which help to protect the environment and the cultivation of land forming part of the recreational landscape, all of which are performed by local farmers in the interests of the general public, should be encouraged and subsidized.
● The local authorities should purchase agricultural land and sell it to interested young farmers.
● Farmers should be paid generous compensation for the right of passage over their land and for lower yields due to funiculars, ski lifts and ski runs.
● Local processing and sale of locally produced food and materials such as timber, stone, wool and regional specialities should be promoted.

- Non-tourist services in the public and private sectors, for example the army, education, public transport, banks, insurance companies, etc., should be transferred from the centre of towns to their outskirts.

Focus on the needs and interests of tourists and locals and co-ordinate them

To harmonize tourist development means, first of all, to unravel the tangle of often conflicting interests and set up clear priorities. The following considerations are based on the ideas of Pierre Lainé.[15]

The various needs and interests manifest themselves on three levels. On the first level are the aims and wishes of those who are directly involved in tourism and have a vested interest in it. There are two sides to this: on the one, we have the interest of the host areas and their population in the preservation of their cultural heritage and the environment while at the same time using the possibilities of tourism for economic and social advancement. On the other side is the interest of generating areas and their population in changing the scene, in discovering and exploring.

On the second level are the aims and interests of people, enterprises and institutions who are professionally interested in the tourist system and in the tourist area itself; the building industry, the catering trade, commercial firms, various services, employers and employees in the sport and entertainment sector, etc. On this level also go the 'intermediaries', who act between supply and demand, such as travel agencies, tourist organizations and the like. Finally come those enterprises whose income does not remain in the destination area, e.g. outside promoters, manufacturers and suppliers of leisure and sports equipment and others.

On the third level are the interests of persons and groups who appear only occasionally and accidentally in the tourist system – real estate dealers or promoters, who only occasionally do business in the tourist trade and then withdraw again are an example of these.

The concept of a balanced tourist development presupposes strict adherence to a hierarchy of objectives: the objectives of the first level – the interests of the host population and of travellers – must be given priority over the objectives of the other levels, i.e. over the interests of the various professional groups. Efforts must be made on this first level to co-ordinate the needs of the locals and tourists and to plan development in such a way as to make the result useful for both parties.

This, in turn, presupposes concerted action; the policies in such action could be worked out at joint consultations, the results of which should be, wherever possible, formulated in long-term contracts regulating the settlement of interests on a binding and enduring basis. In cases of incompatibility or doubt, the interests of the host population must have precedence over those of the outsiders.

Unfortunately, this hierarchy of objectives and priorities is hardly ever observed in practice and the question of compatibility is not even an issue. Worse still: priorities are repeatedly turned upside down. This leads to misguided development and to policies dictated by outside interests: tourism becomes the hoarder of land, nature and the cultural heritage, a new colonizer and destroyer of the environment.

A very good case in point, which will illustrate the tragic consequences of disregard for the hierarchy of objectives and the acceptance, or imposition of false priorities, is the sad example of the building market. Here 'the wheel has come full circle': in many holiday areas the building industry has completely detached itself from tourism and now follows its own laws. In the holiday resorts of the Swiss mountain areas a gigantic flood of chalets, weekend and second homes has been built, with the aim of making a quick profit and without any consideration for the long-term interests of the local communities. Positive estimates of tourist growth prospects, intensive development of the infrastructure by local authorities, the need for investing into property, including foreign investors putting in capital they have taken out of their own countries, and many other factors have led to a construction boom, which is continuing despite the fact that many communities would now like to stop it. 'Service tourism' has been replaced by 'real estate tourism' and the property sector has found itself promoted to that of the most lucrative tourist business. Today many people make their living by selling land – they live off landscape consumption. In the Swiss tourist canton of Wallis, about 20 per cent of the employed population work in the building industry. If the further construction of chalets and holiday flats were prohibited, about 4,000 jobs would be lost, which effectively means that the building must go on. Cantonal official policy says that no more than 1500 new holiday flats per year should be built,[16] but in reality many more will be put up. More building – in order to keep the building industry going. This won't favour tourism, it will act against it. The estimate for Switzerland as a whole until the year 2010 predicts a growth of over one million beds, above all in second and weekend homes. This would require about 150 km² of land, which is roughly double the area of Lake Zurich.[17] The building industry uses the force of circumstances to assert itself. It is strongly represented in administrative bodies at all levels and has a strong lobby. In the eyes of this industry tourist development means: build, build and build again. The likelihood of the building boom being halted, then, is remote, and all the more so if we take into account the fact that in many districts the amount of land set aside for building has been overgenerous, and that the construction industry is already the owner of a large part of it anyway. If all this construction goes ahead, it could easily house twelve million people, double the total population of Switzerland. Another snag to this situation is that most of the building in tourist resorts is done by outside contractors, because the local industry does not have the necessary capacity. The negative effects of this autonomous building market on the locals and tourism are legion: high infrastructural costs for the communes because the supply system and public utilities must be geared to peak demand; low tax revenues; rising property prices; problematic and expensive housing construction for the local population; disfigured villages and landscapes; dead resorts and closed-up shops out of season.

This example shows clearly what has to be done to protect the interests of the locals in holiday areas and safeguard their autonomy from external decision making: *The local population must play the leading role in the struggle for control over the means of production – land, labour and capital*. This demand is of central importance in the following three propositions. In addition to this, if the gap between the needs of travellers and locals is to be reduced, the following two principles must be taken into account:

- *The luxury character of tourism, i.e. of tourist facilities must be reduced. Possibilities for more simplicity without loss of quality are to be investigated* (see the proposition regarding 'emphasizing and cultivating what is typically local').

- *Priority must be given to investment and facilities which equally benefit travellers and locals and can be used by both sides (e.g. infrastructural and leisure facilities).*

Keep control over property in local hands

One of the most important factors in a balanced development is the *principle of local sovereignty in matters concerning the use of land. Local authorities must retain a firm grip on this their most effective instrument of control.*

Land use policy and regional planning policy are the key instruments through which host areas can control tourist development. A policy of laissez-faire and laissez-aller opens the door wide open to land speculation. Development can soon get out of balance and take an incorrigible course to the detriment of the local population. Depending on the country, local authorities have various means at their disposal of retaining control over the use of land. Even where land is in private hands, public authorities are not powerless, but can exercise a crucial influence through regional land-use planning.

In new developments, a local government body should secure control over the land before the first turf is cut. Of course, this applies only to possible construction sites and land which could be used for various tourist activities. The whole development plan will then be worked out together with a partner organization consisting of external promoters, investors, and experts: all modalities concerning the construction, management, financing, promotion and sales will be described in a development contract, which should also specify the exact division of labour and each participant's role. That these are not merely wild theories has been proved by Pierre Lainé with the development of several holiday resorts, based on an integral and contractually regulated partnership.[18]

But even when such comprehensive planning is not or no longer possible, there are at least two guidelines that should be observed: first, *use the given instruments for regional planning to maximum advantage and in a consistent* way, which is seldom the case at present; second: *the terms for co-operation and partnership must be laid down in long-term, binding contracts and conventions* (which is even more rare).

Measures

Below is a list of regional planning measures that can help correct blunders in construction developments in holiday resorts (from a catalogue of demands for Swiss recreational areas):[19]

- Revision of resort planning/restriction of the building area.
- Reduction of building zones (if no public utilities have been provided, there is no compensation liability).
- Reallocation of land: better grouping of land uses – larger unbuilt areas.
- Construction in stages (time and space) in order to prevent dispersed building. Phased development of the infrastructure: staggered building of publicly financed utilities.

- Allocating special zones exclusively for housing developments for the local population (the legal enforceability of this measure has not been clarified yet).
- No new zoning.
- Conclusion of provisional construction waivers with landowners.
- Provisionally prohibited building as a temporary solution.
- More detailed and stricter regulations relating to the architecture of building projects.
- Award of contracts for publicly financed construction to the local building industry only; staggering of public investment.
- Purchase of land by local government for future housing developments for the local population.
- Construction of municipal housing for the local population.
- Enforcement of unbuilt river bank and lake shore protection.
- Gradual reduction of construction activities.

Plan investment in tourist development

Capital investment in tourism must be planned in such a way that both sides – the destination area and representatives of the generating area, must undertake financial obligation and co-responsibility even if not in an equal share. External or foreign investors must participate in the financing of the 'non-profitable' part of tourist facilities (notably the infrastructure and public utilities) and assume a part of the investment risk; on the other hand, local participation in profit – yielding investment (accommodation, catering and entertainment facilities, etc.) must be ensured. The latter can be achieved by developing new ways of financing, e.g. on a co-operative basis. The main objective of this should be to provide opportunities for broad financial participation by the local population.

However, self-reliance in development does not mean that external or foreign capital should necessarily be altogether rejected. On the contrary, there are very good reasons for attracting external capital in tourist development. First of all, the local community would hardly be able to meet the costs from its own funds alone; furthermore, external capital can considerably expand the financial basis and thus make it possible to plan better tourist facilities, which in turn stand a better chance of attracting custom and thus bring more profit to all parties in the long term. But the most convincing argument for attracting external capital is the fact that it is the only way in which generating areas too will participate in the risk inherent in all tourist development.

A person who has invested money in a holiday resort will not simply turn his back on it when he no longer likes it. It is much more probable that he will do his utmost to keep its bookings high even when demand is slack. He would certainly be much less committed if he didn't have any financial interests there. Participation by external promoters in the investment is, then, highly desirable; without it, holidays areas are even more dependent on current fashions and buying power in the areas of tourists' origin and on promoters' whims. There are quite a few examples of tour operators cancelling their bookings at short notice, switching suddenly from one destination to another and deserting some destinations. But there are also positive examples of promoters who have a financial interest in a resort or an area and make great efforts to keep business booming. Therefore: investment of external capital – yes. But carefully planned, contractually regulated and on the condition that the capital never leads to external domination. This can also be prevented by appropriate contractual provisions.

Rely on the local work force – improve job quality

Generally speaking, the development of tourist facilities is appropriate from the local point of view only when the jobs created by it go to the indigenous population of the resort or area. Reliance on labour from outside should be kept to a minimum. It is important that locals be given skilled and managerial jobs, even if this is often possible only after a certain time. It is a fact that many jobs in the tourist trade are not very attractive; the situation should be improved through an intensification of training programmes on all levels and above all through improved working conditions (notably higher wages and better working hours) and the development of social security.

Discussions about tourist development policies usually tend to overlook such questions as recruitment of the work force and job quality. Tourist development projects are hardly ever run by local people. It seems that the natural choice for the good jobs and the demanding managerial posts lies with foreigners and people from the city. The locals are left with the menial jobs and services. Balanced tourist development requires a new attitude: planned efforts aimed at re-evaluating work in the tourist trade and a much stronger local presence on all levels. The partnership we are striving for should manifest itself in job allocation too. Professionals from the host areas must participate in all aspects of the tourist system and in all planning stages: the design, construction and running of facilities as well as in information, publicity and sales. Wouldn't it be a good idea for big travel agencies to have local staff from the host areas working in the advisory service at the desk, designing the information and publicity material, and as travel guides. To show that partnership is not an empty slogan.

Emphasize and cultivate what is typically local

All over the world what tourist brochures offer their prospective customers is as alike as two peas. It is as if local characteristics and traditions were something to be ashamed of and have therefore been touched up, everything being geared to an imaginary and uniform tourist taste. The indigenous culture has been thoughtlessly obliterated and replaced by an impersonal tourist-unculture, thus aiding the worldwide 'Coca-Colonization'. This is no doubt one of the reasons why all tourist destinations have become interchangeable at will and trade rivalry correspondingly greater.

The development which we advocate is based on a clear commitment to local culture: local traditions and characteristics should feature prominently. In this connection we should also remember the proposal for less luxurious tourism and a return to greater simplicity. The architecture in holiday areas should be modelled on the traditional local style using traditional materials and workmanship. Here lies an opportunity, too, to introduce travellers to the local art (murals, etc.). Local food and specialites should be placed at the top of the menu. Occasional 'adjustments' (e.g. less hot pepper or garlic) may be desirable, but need not necessarily detract from the quality of the local cuisine. The appearance of so-called international cuisine on the menu should be reduced to make way for more local dishes. Similarly, preference should be given to domestically produced beverages. The strongly internationalized curricula of hotel-management schools and other vocational training institutions should be revised to place much greater emphasis on the promotion of local features.

The host population in tourist target areas would do well to behave with more confidence and pride and make their rich cultural heritage more accessible to travellers. There are many arguments for the adoption of such a policy, not the least of them being the prospect of better market chances.

One of the principles of successful marketing is that if a product is to become a best seller it should have an unmistakable identity – it should contain a Unique Selling Proposition and stand out among other products. In the international tourist business, where everything follows the same stereotypes, such a policy is long overdue. Furthermore, if local resources rather than imports are relied upon, a larger share of the economic benefit will remain in the host areas. The locals' interest in tourism will be greater and this, in turn, will increase the chances for an encounter with travellers.

The scope for the practical interpretation of these proposals is, of course, very wide, and many people will be sceptical about them. The pursuit of such a policy may be compared to walking the tightrope between genuine and sham folklore, between honesty and falsehood. Some of the difficulties can be seen in, for example, tourist resort architecture, where it is all too easy to slip into a pseudo-country style. The alarming spread of a uniform and clichéd rustic design (which is increasingly invading tourist resorts in the Alpine area) in the service of a fake homeliness, with agricultural implements, wheels and yokes decorating the walls of restaurants and nightclubs, is not an alternative, although there are examples of more successful interpretations. The demand for more local food will certainly provoke the greatest scepticism. The prevalance of international cuisine is defended stubbornly on the grounds that it is the guests who want this kind of food. But have the guests ever been asked what they would like to eat? Have they ever been offered local food and introduced to local traditions? Is it really the tourists' wish to eat no cheese dishes in Switzerland, no lamb in Morocco, no fish or retsina wine in Greece, no curry in India? It is simply not true that most tourists will eat nothing but hamburgers or steak with chips or drink only French wine, German beer or Coca-Cola. Many tourists are already looking for something else. Many others could be easily persuaded to try something they don't yet know – whether it be food or some other new experience. What the tourist expects from the place where he spends his holiday is the sanitary comfort and hygiene to which he is accustomed at home. Apart from that, he is very willing to experiment and grateful for opportunities to do so. This applies especially to the European tourist even more than to the American one. The unimaginative tourist hotch-potch can be neither justified nor excused by referring to the prevailing wishes of the guests.

It may require some courage to pursue this new policy, to do things one's own way and be different from others. But if applied flexibly and consistently, it could invest travel with a new colour and bring tremendous gains to all participants.

14

Ghetto or no ghetto – that is the question

Use the advantages of new artificial holiday centres

As long as the basic conditions of holiday-making remain the same and travel continues to take place in the form of periodic mass exoduses, the development of artificial holiday worlds in the form of large holiday centres is not only necessary but desirable. The principles presented in the proposals that follow should be applied, mutatis mutandis, to the planning and development of such centres.

We must realize that the exodus of millions of people has produced new requirements, which cannot be met by small-scale organizational forms, by manual operation so to speak. This applies not only to transport but equally to accommodation and leisure. Modern tourism cannot be squeezed into small resorts with limited facilities. If everybody is to be given the chance to go on holiday, large-scale accommodation 'stations' – large holiday metropolises – are needed. It is a popular pastime to describe them condescendingly as ghettos, deploring above all the isolation of tourists in an artificial world of illusions. But it is surely more realistic to acknowledge that they are necessary and carefully plan their development instead of letting such structures mushroom in an uncontrolled way, which is already happening in popular tourist regions and will continue to happen. It is only through adequate planning that the important advantages of such tourist centres can be used, namely the regulated relationship to their natural and social environment and the diversified compact supply of experiences they offer the tourist. Tourism in reservations, in 'ghetto-like' centres may be the more 'hygienic' solution, because the destination area can benefit from all the economic advantages, while restricting contact to a limited area and a small circle of people and thus protect itself from the overwhelming ecological and, even more importantly, cultural 'infection'. 'Cultural protection' and 'host population protection' have emerged as new concepts alongside the conservation of nature and landscape. This view of things is by no means eccentric – especially not for developing countries, but it is quite legitimate for our tourist scene as well. In Third World countries such centres should be developed on locations outside the reach of the everyday life of the population in order to avoid the cultural shock.[20]

There is little reason for 'cultural' and educated people to turn their noses up at such forms of holiday-making. Most people who go to such centres don't feel at all that they have been 'sent' to a ghetto. After all, what the majority want is to switch off, to simply recuperate and have a good time with like-minded people, what could be better for it than a holiday centre built for this very purpose, the scene of animated holiday life where loneliness and boredom are unknown. That is quite an achievement in itself, so why not accept it and welcome it!

No general rules about the size of tourist centres can be given. The dimensions can differ widely, depending on the location of the centre and on the principles according to which it has been designed. But what one should certainly expect to find in them is the 'human dimension', a feeling of warmth and security, diversity and holiday centres should never degenerate into gigantic complexes, into anonymous leisure-accommodation machines, treating their 'inmates' like battery hens. A precondition for this is a reduction of metropolitan yardsticks and an increase of architectural diversity. It is a task ridden with difficulties and we are still very far from mastering it worldwide.

Further develop traditional forms of travel and holidays and try out new ones

The future certainly doesn't lie only in the kind of 'colonies' for holiday people that have been described in the preceding proposal. *Diverse forms of travel and holidays must be preserved and even expanded, but they must not be allowed to emerge and grow in an uncontrolled way. Rather they should be part of a planned development, thought out with the participation of all those who have an interest in it. This applies not only to the future development of traditional forms of holiday-making but also to the search for, and experimentation with, new and alternative forms of travel.*

Traditional holiday resorts, in which locals and tourists live in peaceful and, ideally, even friendly, co-existence, are not an anachronism – far from it. There is no doubt that they come closest to what the majority of tourists really want and dream about. Furthermore, it is probably the form of tourism the host population prefers. Whether such resorts will remain viable and worth the experience in the long run, depends on two factors. First, there must be a balanced ratio between the number of tourists and the local population – the locals shouldn't be swamped by crowds of tourists. Just where the limits of the social and psychological carrying capacity lie, however, and the point at which the system may get out of balance, cannot be determined with scientific precision. It is up to the local population to decide what it considers the saturation point. But the decision must be made in time and then be binding. The second condition is that the holiday resort maintains a mixed economic structure and avoids having a 'single-crop' (tourist) economy. (See above.)

Experiments in alternative forms of travel away from the tourist mainstream, are very welcome – but only if they do not deviate from the 'philosophy' that we have tried to outline in the proposals in this book. We should also keep in mind that such forms will always remain the privilege of a minority and that they cannot solve the problems of mass tourism. But some ideas springing from them could perhaps also be used on the level of mainstream tourism.

Here are a few *examples* of the direction the experimenting could go:

• Further development of the so-called 'geographical animation model'.[21] The model, which has already been widely tested in practice, provides an alternative to the usual excursions and sightseeing programmes, that are exactly the same all over the world. The basic idea is to enable tourists to get acquainted with the reality of the country they are visiting and get more involved in their holiday environment. Instead of visiting monuments and classical sights on the well-worn tourist track, listening to cultural and historical explanations, eating tourist menus and shopping for souvenirs, tourists are taken to see the people and their everyday life. For instance, by bus to various villages to visit local factories, see the local chapel with beautiful frescoes, buy bread, cheese and fruit at the local market, try some local food on a farm, go exploring by themselves, pick herbs, go for a swim in between, listen to the parish priest explain about the icons in his church, etc. Geography as an experience and not as a compulsory exercise. According to its initiators, the model can be used everywhere and would appeal to a large number of tourists.

• Proponents of 'social hiking' suggest a development along very similar lines.[22] What was formerly possible for small groups of hikers to do spontaneously, could now be prepared and organized. Groups of tourists would meet with experts or people of the same age or occupational group for talks. From these discussions special sight-seeing and guided tours would be organized.

• Another related proposal is that of a new form of the study trip. Travellers would meet natives of the target country with whom they have something in common and who are interested in an exchange of information. Ideally, the invitation should come from the host country and be followed by an invitation back from the guests. A precondition for the success of such a scheme is that sufficient time should be allowed for discussions and meetings.

• A somewhat different purpose underlines solidarity tourist visits to Third World countries, which is already organized by church circles in Latin America. The initiative for these so-called 'encuentros' can come only from the host country. The idea is to expose people to a life style which is new for them and then give them the opportunity to discuss this situation with their hosts. Visitors live with simple people, sharing their frugal meals and their standard of living. They stay long enough to understand their hosts' feelings, hardships and hopes.[23]

• Holidays on the farm are an alternative of tourism which is gaining popularity in many countries. One of its conceivable components could be a limited amount of participation by the guests in the work of the farm, something which already happens in a number of places.

• Renting rooms from the local population as an alternative to hotel accommodation could perhaps become more widespread when travelling to foreign countries.

• House or flat exchange between inhabitants of different towns or countries has not been widely publicized so far.

• Many other alternatives, which for various reasons cannot be presented here in detail, would be possible. Indeed, to discover and try them out for oneself is one of their characteristics.[24]

It goes without saying that the commercial tourist trade can hardly be expected to promote such forms of travel, because they are labour intensive and therefore of little commercial interest. This is a broad and still largely untapped field of activity for charitable organizations, the church, educational institutions, etc. They should be charged with the task of promoting this desirable expansion of the non-commercial tourist supply.

In looking for alternative forms of tourism we should always be guided by the ambition to reinvest travel with charm and to learn something from other people and cultures without, as is often the case with the current practice, damaging them.

15

Conscious travel – advice and exercises for a different travel behaviour

In chapters 13 and 14 we discussed the principles we thought desirable in creating, planning and structuring the conditions for travel. At this point I want to underline a major reservation: even if we did succeed in improving the external conditions of travel in the direction of our discussions, travel itself would not necessarily become more human. For this to happen the behaviour of all the participants – travellers and their hosts – must be changed. It is on such a change that all my following proposals and all my hopes are based. In the same way, the desired structures will probably be brought about only when progress has been made on this level.

Use the holidays as a time for self-communion

We carry the key to happy leisure, to fulfilling and memorable holidays, to more humanity in travel, like a Field Marshal's baton in the pack. The responsibility cannot be shifted on to the holiday package, the travel guide, the weather, the quality of the food or the dear tourists that surround us. All these elements are more or less marginal for the success of the holiday. It is up to us and our attitude and behaviour whether we win or lose something, whether we build or destroy something. *We must first find our own self; we must learn how we can meet ourselves before we can be expected to be tolerant and considerate toward others.* We must be fully aware of our own selves if we want to understand all the things that surround us. The holidays could be used for establishing this inner balance. They are particularly suited for this because they are self-determined leisure shaped entirely by ourselves.

We must make the effort to understand this and use the chance for 'a holiday leading to oneself' instead of chasing the illusion of 'holidays away from oneself. The belief that one can escape from oneself during the holidays, the idea that half one's personality can be sent away while the other remains at home is absurd. But this is exactly what is put forward by some of the tourist trade advertising. It speaks of the new, the true and different life, of a paradise on earth and people embrace it eagerly, hoping to compensate for what they miss in everyday life. Yet, a short period of holiday happiness, although enjoyed to the full, is merely a soap bubble, which bursts without leaving a trace. What follows is emptiness. To experience fully would mean not to let things just happen to us and then let them drip off, but to absorb them consciously and make them a meaningful part of our personality. It is only then that they leave their mark. Holidays toward the Self: from externally guided tourists to the internally guided (holiday) people. But how can this be done? How can we find the means, when we are surrounded by the smooth and clearly indicated motorways leading to the easily accessible, and seemingly easily digestible, holiday pleasures?

In his book *'Leisure Without Boredom' ('Freizeit ohne Langeweile'),* the theologian and educationalist, Roman Bleistein gives a number of what he calls *'Suggestions for holidays towards the self'.*[25] They are rather like a kind of finger exercise aimed at helping the suppressed soul to break through. They include simple things, nothing revolutionary. But there's much more to them than meets the eye. They point to our own responsibility and suggest practical ways of cheerfully exercising that responsibility. This is why I find them extremely important. I have tried to summarize them in the shortest possible form.

• Play Robinson Crusoe for once. Expose oneself to the elements, experience the wind, the weather, thunder and lightning. Work hard 'for pleasure', sweat for it: in the garden, in the wood, in the field. Overcome exhaustion. Experience an archaic pleasure and one's own sovereignty as a contrast to the self-alienation in everyday life.

• Hike to remove the stress which prevents recuperation. Be composed and relaxed. Breathe deeply and regularly. Make small discoveries along the path. Talk with hiking companions. Take a break. An integral experience.

• Exert yourself physically. Let off steam through extreme physical exertion to free yourself from the daily adaptation to 'economical behaviour', like a bird at last set free from its cage.

• Sleep. For the first three or four days of your holiday surrender to tiredness. Sleep long in order to be able to relax and perceive things, to get into a good mood and become communicative.

- Switch off the time machine. Take off the watch. Get rid of time pressure, the deadline, the agenda. Escape from time. Live a timeless and relaxed day. Catch up with 'natural time'. Look for the sun. Listen to the bells. Observe your own rhythm.
- Regain the ability to be stimulated. Fight against the dull, unresponsive, everyday person. Be stimulated. Perceive and react to signals. The sun, wind, water, smell, heat, cold, optical stimuli, sexual stimuli. Stimulating holidays.
- Learn to observe instead of just looking at and seeing many things in a hurry. Regain the ability to perceive the inconspicuous, the non-exotic, the quiet. Look again at a tree, a flower, a mountain, the sky. Look for a long time, observe and perceive. 'You can only see with your heart. The most important things are invisible to the eye.' (Antoine de Saint-Exupéry.)
- Find happiness in small things instead of wanting more and more. Not the superlative, the most expensive, the extreme. Have an eye for the small joys, for the found and discovered. Find your small holiday booty. Collect rocks, shells, starfish, cones, feathers. Take home your *personal* souvenir.
- Use the chance of 'being together on holiday'. Break the communication barrier. Associate with others instead of passing them by in a hectic hurry and scurry. Discover that 'they' aren't at all like 'that'.
- Share your experiences with others. Travel the world in company, with the family, with a group. Talk and listen, exchange views, joys, fight against isolation and narrow-mindedness.
- Discover your own creative potential, the unsuspected talents slumbering in every person. Cut a pipe, build a water mill, make small masterpieces out of natural materials. Take up drawing, painting or pottery. Creativity makes freedom.
- Use leisure and holidays to meet other people. Have time for others, be there for others, think of others instead of yourself. Play like a father with your small children – the way they like it. Be polite. Touch, feel, hold hands. That intimate encounter. A balance between giving and taking.
- Learn and explore during the holidays – don't just 'go, see and conquer'. Don't always try to find an explanation for everything. Look at things with different eyes. Admire, wonder. Put questions. Be surprised by yourself.
- Reawaken your imagination for play and games, which is suppressed in everyday life. Don't take only the 'beautiful' toy along.

Invent new games. Do charades, sing, play ball, cards, hide-and-seek, compete. Get out of yourself. Be yourself. To play is human and it liberates.

• Open up and be receptive to the various forms of happiness. Useful questions to ask oneself: does happiness for me lie only in extremes, in the exotic, in prestige? Am I already sceptical about happiness? Can I find happiness in small things? In finding a beautiful mushroom. In dashing down hill in powder snow. In a trip with the family. In an hour of meditation. There are, indeed, many little things that can make one happy.

Take a critical consumer attitude

The mature tourist is always a critical consumer – both in everyday life and in making decisions about his holidays. He is discerning in his choices of what to take from the many travel offers and critical toward himself. He analyses, compares and examines before making the decision what to buy. He tries to see through the seductive promises made by tourist publicity. He chooses his travel destination advisedly. He doesn't accept the philosophy of tourist trade competition which says that prices are more important than countries. He considers the consequences that his visit and his behaviour may have, as well as who can benefit from or be damaged by his journey. He doesn't always go for the lowest price, and once there, doesn't always try to pay even less or bargain harder, because he knows that low prices are often the result of exploitation of other people. He applies the idea underlying the action 'jute instead of plastic' to travel. This implies that he chooses those forms of travel which are least harmful to the environment, which are least disturbing for the people and cultures of the tourist areas and from which they get the greatest benefit. He spends his money on those products and services about which he knows the origin and who will profit from their sale. He observes these principles when choosing accommodation, food, means of transport, visiting institutions, buying souvenirs. He takes time to prepare his journey and he stays as long as possible in the places he visits so that the experience may be a lasting one and that he may really identify with it.

The mature tourist resists the thoughtless exploitation and standardization that are part and parcel of the usual tourist business. He opposes the big machine by trying, at least in his personal behaviour, not to exploit but to assume responsibility.

The critical tourist will increasingly find the courage, even during his holidays, to protest against activities which blatantly disregard all these principles. In the long run he will become more and more wary about having to pay the piper and be duped into listening to somebody else's tune.

To promote this critical attitude in tourists should be the first aim of all those who are involved in consumer protection and information in the field of tourism. But their efforts should not centre only on, for instance, the protection of the rights of travellers versus tour operators, they should begin with and emphasize the 'obligations' of travellers, their responsibilities and the ways in which they can learn and acquire a critical consumer behaviour.

Remember some basic rules for more considerate travel

Well-meaning demands for better travel are often lost in wish catalogues so abstractly formulated that the individual has difficulty in translating them and applying them to himself. The problem has, however, been recognized by many authors and institutions committed to the humanization of travel. They have therefore begun translating their ideas into a kind of '*Code of Ethics*', addressed directly to travellers. Below are twelve behaviour proposals suggested by Ron O'Grady in his booklet *Third World Stopover*.[26] They are fairly representative of other similar examples and although primarily intended for travel in developing countries, much of what the proposals advocate applies to tourism in general.

1   Travel in a spirit of humility and with a genuine desire to learn more about the people of your host country.

2   Be sensitively aware of the feelings of other people, thus preventing what might be offensive behaviour on your part. This applies very much to photography.

3   Cultivate the habit of listening and observing, rather than merely hearing and seeing.

4   Realize that often the people in the country you visit have time concepts and thought patterns different from your own; this does not make them inferior, only different.

5   Instead of looking for that 'beach paradise', discover the enrichment of seeing a different way of life, through other eyes.

6   Acquaint yourself with local customs – people will be happy to help you.

7   Instead of the Western practice of knowing all the answers, cultivate the habit of asking questions.

8   Remember that you are only one of the thousands of tourists visiting this country and do not expect special privileges.
9   If you really want your experience to be 'a home away from home', it is foolish to waste money on travelling.
10   When you are shopping, remember that the 'bargain' you obtained was only possible because of the low wages paid to the maker.
11   Do not make promises to people in your host country unless you are certain you can carry them through.
12   Spend time reflecting on your daily experiences in an attempt to deepen your understanding. It has been said that what enriches you may rob and violate others.

Formulated in a different way these principles of considerate travel can look something like the following:[27]

Behave instead of take
Listen instead of hear
Grasp instead of grab
Encounter instead of counter
Experience instead of do
Consider instead of condescend
Laugh with instead of laugh at
Ask instead of answer
Search instead of find.

The proposals for a different behaviour shouldn't be based on the intention to regiment travel and impose even more rules in the existing maze of regulations. Not obeying but taking to heart should be their purpose. It would certainly be naive to believe that such proposals can have a strong and immediate impact on tourist behaviour. But this kind of discussion can initiate new thinking and lead to a more criticial attitude to one's own tourist role even among those people who are usually not inclined to occupy themselves intellectually with tourism.

Efforts must therefore be made to develop such initiatives and 'market' them with a professionalism equal to that of more commercial tourist agencies. Again, the first step must come from the non-commercial sector, but if this new approach is to be effective and become widespread, the co-operation with the commercial sector is indispensable. Every tourist should be expected in a figurative or literal sense – to sign the 'Charter for Considerate Travel' and join the 'Club of Responsible Tourists'. The observance of the 'ten commandments for socially and environmentally compatible travel' must become a matter of honour. Commitment to the idea could be expressed by a sticker on the windscreen or some other external sign. After this 'gentle' pressure for joining the cause, social control mechanisms begin to function. Idealistic you say. Is it?

Exercise moderation in travel: less far – less changes – less often – stay at home from time to time

A part of more conscious travel is the consideration whether less often would possibly mean more.

Do not always travel so far: for many people it would be better and more restful if they spent their holidays and leisure somewhere closer to their homes. The good need not be synonymous with the distant. Many surprising, exciting and even exotic things can be discovered in our immediate surroundings, if we only take the trouble to look for them, if we try to observe the habitual with an eye for the unusual. Perhaps we have too exotic expectations when we go on holiday to distant countries and often try to fulfil them in an artificial way. This often leads to less excitement than we had hoped for and may even be disappointing. To travel less far means to reconcile leisure and wanderlust. Many people turn their holidays into a caricature of leisure: they apply to them a kind of economic performance principle which they have adopted in everyday life. For them holidays mean doing as many miles on as little money as possible, going as far as they can while spending a minimum of time and money. We can have real leisure only if we take our time and are ready to see less and go less far.

Change the travel destination less often: there are people who follow the performance principle even in their leisure and collect travel destinations like stamps to be put into the photo album. This kind of breathless travel should be replaced by greater destination loyalty: travel more often, or even regularly, to the same place. Only in this way can we develop a true relationship to a country and its people. We can meet the local population and they can meet us. The anonymous tourist becomes a welcome guest. Experience shows that holiday-making in the same place also fosters relationships among tourists. Meeting year after year, holiday-makers become friends. Destination-loyal tourists are also much more likely to feel that they must protect and embellish the holiday area because they become interested in it, its fate concerns them. Those merely passing through show indifference in this respect. We should ask ourselves why children always want to go back to the same place. Especially destination-loyal are the elderly, who realize that the best place to recuperate and relax is a place known to us: it is there that we feel safe, it is like a refuge from which we can venture out to new experiences if we want to but to which we always return with pleasure.

Travel less, stay at home from time to time: conscious travel can also mean deciding not to go away for once and spending the weekend or the holidays at home. At a time when going away for the weekend or the holidays has become a matter of course, we should ask ourselves more often the seemingly banal question: why am I going away? And we would then have to admit that we don't necessarily have to go on a trip to recuperate or get a change of scene, both of which may sometimes be done equally well or even better at home or in its immediate vicinity. This possibility is ignored because travel has become an automatism, a kind of habitual mobility and also because it is sometimes infinitely more difficult to be inventive and take the initiative at home than to simply get into the car, board the train, catch the plane and leave. It is the headless 'simply-taking-off'. If we stayed at home more frequently and travelled less often, travel would surely regain some of its quality of a rare and exciting experience which we eagerly await and look forward to. Travel to distant countries should most certainly be such an event: a climax, which is not taken for granted and which does not happen necessarily every year.

There is one thing that shouldn't be overlooked: the decision not to travel and to spend free time at home will come easiest to people who live in good residential areas and have a beautiful home. If occasional abstinence from travel for everyone is to become a serious proposition, we must first change and improve general living conditions and humanize everyday life, work, and leisure, thus making travel less necessary as a means for recuperation and regeneration. Of course, there are many people who have no choice at all. Whether they want to or not, they must spend their holidays at home either because they cannot afford anything else or are bound to their place of residence in some other way. For many of them staying at home means an impoverishment to life rather than the enrichment it can bring those who have the choice. To comfort the unwilling home-holiday-makers (or non-holiday-makers) with the notion that there are many fascinating things they can do there would be pure cynicism. But for others it does make sense to advocate relaxation and leisure at home coupled with domestic sightseeing as an occasional alternative.

In any large town there are countless possibilities for spending a two-week holiday – or even longer – in a pleasant, adventurous and enriching way. We can go sightseeing in our own city, for more often than not we know it less well than tourists; we can explore a neighbouring town or village; we can make use of swimming pools, walks and parks, visit museums and look at monuments. There are many things we can do in the house for which we would otherwise not have time; listening to music, indulging in hobbies, playing with the family. We can even change the function of rooms for once: sleep on the floor in the living room, have breakfast in the bathtub. We can swap family roles: the father does the cooking, the mother reads the paper. Just for a change we can turn a day into night and night into day. We can undertake something with others who have not gone away. Wouldn't enriching holidays at home illuminate our everyday life more than a brief stay in a foreign environment?

Municipal policies should do more for those who spend their holidays at home. People who travel can enjoy the many facilities and services offered by the tourist industry, but for those who stay at home no comparable efforts are made. The leisure and cultural policy of towns and communes has to fill this gap and do much more than is now the case. Imaginative encouragement and information about the many leisure possibilities of holidays at home are perhaps even more important than a good leisure infrastructure. But such activities have so far been sadly neglected.

A total abstention from travel, which is demanded by some critics as a reaction to the negative consequences of tourism, is not what I am advocating. Such a policy would – among many other things – rob us of the great chance of personal development offered by travel. Staying at home can never replace and satisfy the longing for distant places. But occasional holidays at home can shed a new light on many things.

16

School for a more human tourism

Opt for an honest and responsible marketing of tourism

This demand is addressed to all those who organize, offer, sell and inform about travel – what we might call 'the producers of holidays'. Even if they are reluctant to accept the fact, it is certainly true that many of them – especially the most powerful among their members – have an incomparably greater influence on consumers than producers in other branches of the economy. They must therefore assume a special responsibility. Most tourists are unsure consumers. They have many wishes and longings, but rarely a clear picture of what they really want and can therefore be easily influenced. The majority are still passively receptive, open and willing consumers, ready to be led. They are grateful for help, advice and concrete offers, indeed, they rely on them. They put their faith in their helpers. Big tour operators, therefore, not only shape tourism but opinions as well. The ultimate pace of tourism depends to a large extent on their business policy and their marketing. The school for a more human tourism must therefore start with them. They have a special responsibility not only because of the influence they exercise but because – unlike industries producing material goods – they deal in people, cultures, landscapes and in what is becoming one of man's most precious possessions – leisure time.

No supplier in the tourist trade, be he a tour operator, hotelier, carrier or tourist office manager, should try to shirk this responsibility by pretending to act according to customer desires. So many tour operators profess that their only ambition is to satisfy them as quickly, fully and professionally as possible. 'We merely make the arrangements the customer wants', they say. It is a very comfortable shield, behind which it is easy to live and do business without accepting responsibility for the effects of those selfsame arrangements.

I want to call on all suppliers of tourist services to acknowledge their responsibility towards travellers, the host population and the tourist environment, to state clearly what contribution they are prepared to make to a more human tourism and what regulations they are willing to observe. I propose that they should formulate and make public a code of practice and the principles of their internal and external business conduct. Not in a few beautifully worded and vague sentences but in concrete and practicable policy statements, to which they would be answerable.

The laying out of a clear business policy could perhaps restore the partly dented credibility of the tourist business and correct the impression that it is geared, from top to bottom, to profit at any price. It is a highly suspect alibi when representatives of big tour operators present very open-minded arguments at seminars critical of travel in Third World countries or when they subsidize studies and research into how to achieve better tourism, while some of them, more or less openly, advertise sex trips to Bangkok (or organize them on request). What is needed are not only fine words but corresponding action.

For this action to have a wider impact, professional tourist trade associations should consider the possibility of adopting common business principles which would serve as guidelines or even be binding on all members. A 'Moral Code' for travel agencies for instance, laying down the principles of co-operation with the suppliers (conditions for making contracts and such like), the selection of destinations, pricing policy, advertising, sales, information and liability to travellers and partner firms. A kind of self-supervision of business practices.

A more honest travel marketing would also mean making advertising more informative. Advertising should not appeal only to the escape motives in travellers, extolling tourist destinations as a paradise on earth. They should reflect an effort to present reality and arouse the travellers' interest in it, without forgetting their responsibility as visitors. Tourist oganizations in holiday areas can make a significant contribution to better information by refraining from clichéd advertising and by supplying their partners with authentic information.

Provide better and more comprehensive training for tourist trade personnel

An important precondition for a more human tourism is that all those who are in charge of the travel business should have a broad 'humanistic education'. The narrowly conceived vocational training in tourism must be given a new dimension, which may be called 'tourism ethics'. Students should be introduced to all the determining components of travel and the relationships between them: economy, psychology, sociology, education, geography, ecology of travel: they should realize the obligations and responsibilities of man – an environment-oriented tourism.

As with many other areas, training in the traditional tourist trade occupations is based almost exclusively on courses in technical and business know-how. The usual yardsticks for professional success are quantitative values: more bookings, more arrivals, more excursions, higher sales. It is to these short-term values that the entire professional training and activity is geared. Anything that doesn't directly contribute to the attainment of these goals, including important long-term issues, seems to be nobody's concern. In this approach, the hotelier is a mere 'soup salesman' and the manager of a tourism office a producer of overnight stays. Such a one-sided interpretation of the role and responsibilities of tourist trade personnel is one of the reasons for many misguided tourism developments. What we need in the future, then, are more generalists and fewer specialists. *The training for many occupations in tourism should be redesigned and expanded, its basic elements revised and professional standards upgraded.* In addition to improved qualifications for most traditional jobs, in tourism, new training courses should be created. We are referring, in particular, to the training of leisure and holiday pedagogues; they will be in charge of animation in the leisure world of tomorrow, providing guidance for meaningful and enriching leisure in both home and foreign environments.

Encourage holiday-makers to try new experiences and behaviour

Most people need some help from outside to discover and use their own capacity for having enjoyable and fulfilling holidays. *Action for more human tourism must therefore also awaken and harness the great latent potential in every individual. This difficult but immensely important task could be tackled by developing the right kind of 'animation', that is, encouragement interpreted as guidance to more enlightened travel. This development should go in three main directions: animation as help to self-realization, as help in establishing contact with other tourists and as help in establishing contact with the host population and the host area. Animation should be conducted by trained animateurs, whose personal characteristics (modesty, empathy, etc.) and training must be of the highest professional standards.* This kind of animation is still much too rare in tourism, and when it does occur it is in commercialized and adulterated forms.

It was in 1975 that the Starnberg Study Group for Tourism worked out a comprehensive scheme, proposing six areas of animation. In order to show the wide range of possibilities they offer, we are listing here the proposed areas and the activities they include. We hope that the almost irresponsible summariness of the presentation will not obscure the complexity and ingeniousness of the proposal.[28]

Movement
For example sport: swimming, calisthenics, judo, mountain climbing, hiking. Games: table tennis, ball games, relay games.

Social life
For example picnics, brunch and buffet meals with music, rotating seating order at meals, joining in the celebration of regional and national events, thematic festivities, children's parties, birthday parties.

Creative activities
For example drawing, finger painting, collages, silhouette cutting, enamelling, batik and fabric painting, photography, pottery, request concerts, storytelling, sketching, amateur theatre.

Education, discovery and experience
For example concerts, poetry readings, quizzes, lectures on the history of the host country, beginners' courses in the language of the host country, cooking courses, visits to local farms, paper chases with questions about the land and people, discussions with host country personalities.

Adventure
For example camp fires, bivouacking, night hiking, diving, rafting, rubber dinghy outings, exploring old ruins.

Quiet, self-discovery
For example yoga, listening to classical music, hikes with exploration of details, conversation evenings with a few friends, poetry and prose recitals, story hours for children.

Since the conception of 'animation' is very often misinterpreted in tourism, I should like to make some additional comments and explanations.

People who have travelled a great deal and have observed the travel scene and themselves critically, will have noticed how helpless and lonely many holiday-makers are in their new environment. They have difficulty in establishing contact or in doing something different from what they are used to at home. It seems that the sudden freedom presents a problem. Everyday life has produced too many blocks and inhibitions and repressed interests. It is here that 'animation' can help overcome the obstacles and inhibitions which stand in the way of the desire for more self-development during the holidays. It is important to note in this context that people are very willing and ready to make an effort themselves. We know from practical experience that holiday-makers feel disappointed when, due to misplaced solicitude, they are spoon-fed and expected to be only passive consumers. Effort brings its own rewards and enhances enjoyment.

Properly interpreted 'animation' means: giving a person the courage to come out of his shell; laying free what is buried; providing information, ideas and stimuli; creating favourable preconditions and setting an example; liberate freedom in people, namely the freedom to become active oneself. Animation should help remove barriers, it should encourage the exploratory spirit and openness for new contacts, thus making it possible to escape from isolation. Animation is help towards self-help, stimulation of self-creativity and self-participation. Viewed in this light, animation is an activity whose ultimate goal is to make itself redundant and be replaced by self-animation. It cannot and should not be more than that. The most important task is reserved for those who are being animated.

Animation should not mean: manipulation in the form of planning other people's needs and activities leading to the creation of a new form of dependence. Neither is it necessary for it to be the great spectacle and circus – organized, for example, by various holiday clubs – which one soon sees through and gets tired of. Opinion polls taken in such clubs show that between 30 and 40 per cent of the club guests find the hullabaloo irritating at some time or another.[29]

The animateur is neither a clowning jester nor a showman or super-athlete. He is above all a pedagogue: he is, not merely a teacher, however, but also a learner. How demanding his task is can be seen from the list of requirements formulated by the leisure pedagogue Horst Opaschowski.[30]

'The animateur should have the ability of going up to people, of talking to them, of encouraging social contacts among people and of helping them to become active and creative. If there existed something like a Hippocratic oath for animateurs, it would read as follows:

- Never act against the interests of your vis-à-vis.
- Treat every person as your partner.
- Give people to understand that for you fears and inhibitions are human.
- Take every participant for what he is. Encourage his strengths and do not expect him to conceal his weaknesses.
- Try to make the best use of each person's inclinations, interests and abilities.
- Credit every person with ability, knowledge and independent decision making.
- Help him to identify his needs and interests and to pursue them on his own.'

Inform the host population about tourists and the problems involved in tourism

By supplying the host population with comprehensive information about tourists and tourism, many misunderstandings could be eliminated, feelings of aggression prevented, more sympathetic attitudes developed and a better basis for hospitality and contact with tourists created.

Such information should aim at introducing the host population – initially, all those who come into direct contact with tourists, but also the public at large – to the tourists' background: their country, their daily life (working and housing conditions, etc.), their reasons for travelling and their behaviour patterns. This also includes the presentation of both the advantages and the disadvantages and danger brought about by tourism. The means and channels of information have to be adapted to the needs of the various target groups. Ideally, tourist generating and receiving areas should co-operate in designing the information material.

Although this is certainly an important requirement for all travel areas – both traditional holiday resorts and Third World tourist areas – very little has been undertaken along these lines so far. For example, if a village school teacher in a Swiss tourist resort wants to tell his pupils something about tourists, who are the main source of income for the whole village, he has no teaching materials designed for the purpose. On the other hand, many school teachers are perhaps not even aware of the need to include such information in the curriculum. It is probably also true that the topic wasn't felt to be sufficiently important during their teacher training.

There are a few examples of campaigns through which national tourist offices have tried to make their fellow citizens more sympathetic to tourists and to highlight the economic importance of tourism (e.g. Italy, Spain, Denmark). The importance of taking steps aimed at raising the local population's awareness of tourism has been repeatedly emphasized by representatives of the tourist trade in many other countries as well. However, people usually forget that improved information alone cannot create greater sympathy toward tourism, not to mention an identification with its cause. Information will only take root when the structures of tourism have been improved along the lines suggested in our proposals. As long as no action is undertaken in this sense and the locals feel that the disadvantages of tourism outweigh the advantages, even the best information will fail to produce more understanding and tolerance in the host population.

The following two examples from developing countries should illustrate the manifold possibilities of information.

Example 1:   The curriculum of the hotel school in Nairobi, Kenya, includes a course which tries to find answers to four questions: Who am I? – my country, our culture, our problems, our will. Who are they? – the tourists, their everyday life, how hard some of them have to work for their holidays, their desires, their behaviour. What am I in the eyes of the tourists? – the local, the black, the servant, etc. How can the problems created by various preconceived ideas be solved? – behaviour vis-à-vis tourists etc. Discussions are based on the presentation of didactically designed slide shows.

Example 2:   Suggested by an ethnologist.[31] Pupils from industrialized countries write essays and make drawings, photo-reports and collages describing everyday life in our part of the world with its problems and needs. The material is collected together in exhibitions and shown in the tourist destination areas.

The information of the host population is a broad unexplored field in tourism, ripe for research, education and policy studies.

Learn how to travel – prepare and educate people for travel

Millions of people travel now who don't know the first thing about it. They visit countries, areas, landscapes and cultures without the slightest knowledge about, or preparation for, the new environment; they know nothing about the effects of travel and are not prepared to make a conscious effort to understand the people in the areas they visit. Nor do they actually use the great opportunities inherent in travel – or only a very small part of them. Worst of all, they do a great deal of damage, mainly out of ignorance. What can be expected of a tourist whose preparation for travel consists in buying suntan lotion and malaria tablets! We have never been taught how to use this new mobility which is called tourism. What we have been taught since our childhood is sedentariness: We learn to read, to write, to do the shopping, to drive, etc. But did we ever learn how to travel? This great educational deficiency is responsible not only for much of the wrong behaviour during the holidays but also for disappointments and untapped holiday happiness.

The attempt to make travel itself a largely educational enterprise would not be a sound or feasible policy. It would be unjust to demand that tourists should engage in a compulsory learning process during their holidays, for this is the time when people should have the freedom to do what they like. The educational activity must take place largely at home.

The most efficient causal therapy for a more human tourism is probably the possibility for people to learn the 'art' of travelling from scratch. *I therefore propose the launching of a 'Learn to Travel Campaign', a comprehensive scheme, oriented towards the future and with the active participation of all those who can actively contribute to the process of education. The development of such a campaign requires great effort and even more time. It will take years until it produces its full effect, but the new generations of enlightened travellers will have made it worthwhile. The task should therefore be taken in hand urgently and at all levels.*

The first and most important exponent of the Learn to Travel campaign is *the public educational system*. Starting in the primary school and continuing to university, courses on leisure and travel must become part of all school curricula, the more so because these areas will be even more important in the future than they are today. The pupil should learn, step by step, how to be a tourist. Pierre Lainé has also considered this problem and proposed some ways of how it may be tackled.[32] The first stage of such courses should consist in the exploration of the various rhythms of life: rest, action, leisure, work and their interrelationships. During the next stage the student learns to observe, to understand and to respect nature and the life styles of others. Geography and history as exploration of areas and places where things happen and where other people live. The training will start with short trips aimed at developing the feeling for time and space and awakening an interest in ecology, biology and other areas of science. The learning of foreign languages will play an increasingly important role. At the age of twelve or fourteen the young will have adopted the basic attitudes and behaviour. This initial stage will be followed by in-depth study, beginning with the economic, social and cultural relations between the generating and the receiving areas. At the end of their school education, young people will have obtained a general certificate, a tourist diploma – figuratively speaking, of course. They will have learned how to travel – or the theory behind it. Practical training and experience, as well as further studies, can follow. The more people are trained from their early childhood to be enlightened tourists, the richer and more diversified holiday-making and travelling will become.

Horst Opaschowski has also put forward an interesting proposal for restructuring the school curriculum:[33] Pupils should be given one free period a day, together with their teacher, which they would use for activities of their own choice. By learning to take the initiative and do things together they will learn how to plan and design their leisure independently. In other words, they will be encouraged to become active and make independent decisions. The free period scheme means, in educational terms, just five periods a week less for conventional teaching and about 15 per cent less time for planned preparation for the world of work – the gain must be an efficient preparation for life in general. It goes without saying that the implementation of this proposal would have a positive influence on more conscious travel.

The second important 'activist' group in the Learn to Travel campaign should be the numerous *adult education institutions*. An increasing number of adults, especially older people, are eager to improve and continue their education. An increasing number of educational institutions already cater to their needs and could serve a most useful role in the awareness training of those who have already left school.

A powerful group with great influence over public opinion includes within it institutions such as the *church, political parties, trade unions, cultural societies*, and *consumer organizations*. Some of the strongest consumer organizations, in terms of membership, are the big automobile clubs, whose participation in the scheme I consider particularly important. But all these organizations and institutions should not simply try to imitate commercial travel agencies and organize tours, as some of them do in a rather amateurish way. Rather, they should try to use all the available resources to provide travel guidance and counselling for their members. Regrettably, many of the above mentioned institutions have so far either ignored or paid very little attention to problems related to leisure and travel. As if problems didn't exist in these areas!

If the campaign is to have a broad impact, the *mass media*, especially *television*, must get interested in it. Television programmes are particularly suited to the presentation of ideas for creative and stimulating leisure. Yet, it has so far displayed very little interest in this area – as if it was afraid that by showing people how to spend leisure in a more creative way it would make itself redundant. A few documentaries critical of present-day tourist practice are a step in the right direction, but this is certainly not an achievement in line with the significance travel and holidays have for people today.

The *official tourism organizations* – from the local to the national level – should supply the other participants in the scheme with information material, co-operate in the designing of teaching materials and engage actively in efforts aimed at making travel publicity more objective.

The *commercial tourism sector* should also become involved in the scheme. But they should certainly not be expected to do the lion's share of the work. Ideally, prospective travellers would get information through other channels before calling on the services of a travel agency. The agencies can, nevertheless, make an important contribution, although they would be right in not seeing the education of their customers as their primary task. There have been a few modest efforts on the part of the commercial sector to go beyond mere travel advertising, for example the co-financing of country magazines – called 'Sympathiemagazine' in Germany – which provide a great deal of objective information on travel destinations.[34] Another laudable effort is the subsidizing of documentaries dealing with the problems of Third World travel, amongst other things, which are shown to travellers during flights to these destinations.[35] These two remarkable initiatives have both come from the Starnberg Study Group for Tourism and it is to be hoped that they will be developed further and imitated. The commercial sector can certainly do much more than hitherto. It will probably be prepared to do so when it feels that the other participants in the scheme we have described have become very active and that it can no longer afford not to join them. The great turning point will come when informed tourists take to the road and simply demand a re-orientation of commercial policies.

Last but not least, it should be demanded that *leisure and tourism research* involves itself in the Learn to Travel campaign. So far it has done very little in this respect and has been orientated mainly towards theoretical research into the fundamentals and problems of the commercial sector, which, as is well known, provides part of the research funds. But what use are the most beautifully formulated and interesting findings if they are left sitting on bookshelves or lying idle in drawers. Leisure and tourism researchers should be called upon to make the results of their work available to other participants in the campaign and to co-operate with them in preparing the information material specially designed for each target group. We are pointing this out because if the educational institutions and organizations we mentioned in our list were to join the campaign today, they would largely lack the necessary course and teaching materials. Leisure and tourism research can make an important contribution to filling this gap and thus help to get the educational work under way.

I want to conclude this book with the pledge that I will dedicate myself to the achievement of these goals. Rather than make demands, I want to engage in concrete and positive action. Rather than satisfy myself with research, I want to see actual changes. This book may be taken as the first step in fulfilling these aims.

*   *   *

The key to the humanization of travel is the new, all-round individual. Not just a holiday-person but a human being, aware of himself (and of others) and of his travel motives and desires; one who has learned to be self-critical and to use his experience of other cultures to see himself in a new light. This person will have undertaken, or be prepared to undertake, what we may call an inner journey, on the way acquiring knowledge, humility and a willingness to share these qualities. Only then shall we be able to bring to travel more humanity.

References

Introduction

Seneca, Epistel XXVIII, On Travel as a Cure for Discontent.

1 *Wirtschaftswoche*, No. 16, 1979, Düsseldorf, p. 38.
2 Deutsche Strassenliga und Deutsche Gesellschaft für Freizeit (ed.), *Freizeit und Strasse: Aktive Freizeitgestaltung und Verkehr* (Köln: Druckhaus Müller, 1980), p. 56.
3 Beratende Kommission für Fremdenverkehr des Bundesrates, *Das Schweizerische Tourismuskonzept* (Bern: EDMZ, 1979), p. 54.
4 H. Kahn, *Die Zukunft der Welt* (1980–2000) (Wien, München, Zürich, New York: Verlag Fritz Molden, 1980), pp. 297–8.
5 P. E. Stössl, Leben? In: *Lesebuch 4. Freizeit*, Friesel *et al*, eds. (München: Timm, 1973).
6 Concerning criticism of tourism, see, for example, H. R. Scherrieb, *Der westeuropäische Massentourismus* (Würzburg: Institut für Fremdenverkehrs – und Freizeitforschung, 1974), pp. 51–65.
7 T. Chorherr, *Der Freizeitschock* (Wien, München, Zürich, New York: Verlag Fritz Molden, 1980), p. 132.
8 E. Eppler, M. Ende, H. Tächl, *Phantasie/Kultur/Politik – Protokoll eines Gesprächs* (Stuttgart: Edition Weitbrecht, 1982), p. 21.
9 E. Bloch, *Das Prinzip Hoffnung* (Frankfurt: Suhrkamp Verlag, 1968).

Part One: The Model of Life in Industrial Society
Work – Home – Free Time – Travel

E. Eppler, M. Ende, H. Tächl, *op cit.*, pp. 69–70.

Chapter 1

1 M. Rotach, S. Mauch, P. Güller (eds.), *Szenarien künftiger Entwicklungen* (Bern: Programmleitung NFP 'Regionalprobleme', 1982).
2 *Ibid.*, p. 47.
3 H. C. Binswanger, W. Geissberger, T. Ginsburg, *Wege aus der Wohlstandsfalle* (Frankfurt: Fischer Taschenbuch Verlag, 1983), pp. 34–5.

Chapter 2

4 H. Hamm, Grenzen des Wohlfahrtsstaates, in: *Striftenreihe des Vororts*, No. 31, Vorort (ed.) (Zürich: Vorort, 1982), p. 16.

5 J. Krippendorf, Fehlentwicklungen im Schweizer Tourismus. In: *Schweizer Tourismus – Weichen für die Zukunft richtig gestellt?* Schweizer. Fremdenverkehrsverband (ed.) (Bern, Hallwag, 1983), pp. 27–32.

6 A. Gorz, *Abschied vom Proletariat* (Frankfurt: Europäische Verlagsanstalt, 1980), p. 111.

7 *Ibid.*, p. 130.

Chapter 3

8 R. Kaiser (ed.), *Global 2000 (The Global 2000 Report to the President)* (Frankfurt: Zweitausendeins, 1980), p. 25.

9 E. Fromm, *Die Revolution der Hoffnung* (Frankfurt-Berlin-Wien: Ullstein Verlag, n.d.), p. 13.

10 M. Ferguson, *Die sanfte Verschwörung (The Aquarian Conspiracy)* (Basel: Sphinx Verlag, 1982), p. 85.

11 UNEP/UNCTAD, Die Erklärung von Cocoyoc (The Cocoyoc Declaration). In: *Handbuch für internationale Zusammenarbeit*, Vereinigung für Entwicklungszusammenarbeit (ed.) (Baden-Baden: Nemos Verlag, 1975), pp. 7–8.

Part Two: The Holiday Machine

Chapter 4

1 K. D. Hartmann, quoted by P. Rieger, Die historische und psychologische Dimension – Warum reiste man früher? Warum reisen wir heute? In: *Tourismus – das Phänomen des Reisens, Hermann Ringeling*, Maja Svilar (eds.) (Bern: Verlag Paul Haupt, 1982), p. 15.

2 *Ibid.*, p. 17.

3 T. Chorherr, *op. cit.*, p. 58.

4 K. Marti, *'Heil Vetia'* (Basel: Lenos Verlag, 1981).

5 Edited by Jungfermansche Verlagsbuchhandlung in Paderborn.

6 R. O'Grady in: *KEM Pressedienst – Artikeldienst*, No. 33/1980 (27.10.1980, Basel).

7 K. D. Hartmann, *Zur Gestaltung von Titelseiten auf Urlaubskatalogen*, quoted by: Neues Reisen, Gruppe Neues Reisen (ed.) (Berlin: Gruppe Neues Reisen, 1982), pp. 8–11.

8 S. Hömberg, Reisen zwischen Kritik und Analyse, Zum Stand der Tourismusforschung. In: *Zeitschrift für Kulturaustausch*, No. 3/1978, Michael Rehs (ed.) (Tübingen: Horst Erdmann Verlag, 1978), p. 39.

9 Studienkreis für Tourismus (ed.), *Urlaubsreisen 1986* (Starnberg: Studienkreis für Tourismus e. V., 1987), p. 29.

10 M. Franke, Freizeit in diesem Jahrzehnt – sozialhygienisch gesehen. In: *Schriftenreihe für ländliche Sozialfragen* (Hannover: Verlag M. & H. Schaper, 1973), pp. 18–21.

11 P. Rieger, *Die historische und psychologische Dimension . . ., op. cit.,* p. 14.

12 P. Braunschweig, quoted by U. Mäder, *Fluchthelfer Tourismus – Wärme in der Ferne?* (Zürich: rotpunktverlag, 1982).

13 R. Schober, quoted by F. A. Wagner, Geborgen in der donnernden Ferienherde. In: *Frankfurter Allgemeine Zeitung*, No. 65/1981.

14 A. Vielhaber, P. Aderhold, *Tourismus in Entwicklungsländer* (Bonn: Bundesministerium für wirtschaftliche Zusammenarbeit, 1981).

15 P. Rieger, *Die historische und psychologische Dimension . . ., op. cit.,* pp. 15–17.

16 K. D. Hartmann, quoted by P. Rieger, *ibid.,* p. 15.

Chapter 5

17 Studienkreis für Tourismus (ed.), *Urlaubsreisen 1986, op. cit.,* p. 63.

18 Der Spiegel, *Stress im Urlaub*, No. 33/1978, Hamburg, pp. 36–42.

19 P. Rieger, *Glücklicher Urlaub – Erfahrungen und Ratschläge für den 'inneren' Menschen* (München: Claudius-Verlag, 1982), p. 22.

20 K. Finger, B. Gayler, H. Hahn, K. D. Hartmann, *Animation im Urlaub* (Starnberg: Studienkreis für Tourismus e. V., 1975), p. 71.

21 *Der Fremdenverkehr*, No. 11/1979, Darmstadt, p. 29.

22 H. Hachmann, So eng darf man das nicht sehen. In: *touristik aktuell*, No. 33/1979, Darmstadt, pp. 8–9.

23 P. Rieger, Das grösste Urlaubstheater der Welt – Beobachtungen im Club Méditerranée. In: *Süddeutsche Zeitung*, No. 219/1981, München, p. 45.

24 N. Hug, *Introduction to the Trekkingkatalog 1981* by Inter-Track, Appenzell, 1981.

25 R. Renschler, *Wochen-Zeitung*, No. 0/1981, Zürich.

26 *touristik aktuell*, No. 46/1979, Darmstadt, p. 6.

27 N. Hug, *Introduction to the Trekkingkatalog 1981 . . ., op. cit.*

28 J. Hénard, Den Feind wie seinen besten Freund empfangen. In: *Frankfurter Allgemeine Zeitung*, No. 64/1983, p. R1.

29 *Ibid.*

Chapter 6

30 Chora Sfakion – Insel auf der Insel/Die touristische Bezwingung eines Widerstandsnetzes, quoted by B. Joerges, D. Karsten, Tourismus und Kulturwandel. In: *Zeitschrift für Kulturaustausch*, No. 3/1978, *op. cit.,* p. 10.

31   V. Haas, *The Impact of Mass Tourism on a Rural Community in the Swiss Alps* (Savognin) (Michigan: The University of Michigan, 1976).
32   H. G. Schmidt, Ausverkauf. Oekonomische und sozialpsychologische Aspekte des Tourismus in Entwicklungsländern. In: *Reisen und Tourismus*, R. Schmitz-Scherzer (ed.) (Darmstadt: Dr. Dietrich Steinkopff, 1975), p. 57.
33   L. Fromer, quoted by E. Reinhardt, Entwicklung von Ferienorten, *Die Beteiligung der Ortsansässigen* (Bern: Schweiz. Vereinigung für Landesplanung, 1982), p. 2.
34   E. Meyrat-Schlee, *Bedeutung und Wirkungsweise des kulturellnormativen Systems für die Entwicklung einer Berggemeinde* (Testgebiet Grindelwald) (Bern: Bundesamt für Umweltschutz, 1983), pp. 124–7.
35   Europäische Raumordnungsministerkonferenz, *Beiträge zur Abklärung von Grundsatzfragen der Belastung und der Belastbarkeit im Alpenraum* (Wien: Oesterr. Institut für Raumplanung, 1978), pp. 7–14.
36   P. Lainé, *Libérons le tourisme!* (Paris, éditions fayolle, 1980), pp. 98–102.
37   J. Bugnicourt, Sex – Sonne – Sand, Tourismus zwischen Entdeckung und Eroberung. In: *Informationen*, 29/30, Evangelischer Arbeitskreis Freizeit und Erholung (ed.), Stuttgart, 1983, p. 30.

Chapter 7

38   W. Hunziker, Die menschlichen Beziehungen in der touristischen Entwicklungshilfe. In: *Revue de tourisme*, No. 3/1961, Bern, 1961, p. 90.
39   F. A. Wagner, *Die Urlaubswelt von morgen* (Düsseldorf-Köln: Eugen Diederichs Verlag, 1970), p. 214.
40   E. Meyrat-Schlee, *op. cit.*, p. 122.
41   R. Renschler, Die anthropologische Dimension – Bedrohung oder Erweiterung der Identität von Gast und Gastgeber. In: *Das Phänomen des Reisens, op. cit.*, p. 79.
42   *Ibid.*, p. 80.
43   A. Bouhdiba, Massentourismus und kulturelle Tradition. In: *Unesco-Kurier*, No. 2/1981, p. 7.
44   J. Bugnicourt, *op. cit.*, p. 31.
45   Quoted by P. Fuhrimann, Sind wir wirklich nur 'Sightseer'? In: *Balair-Bordzeitung*, No. 24/1982, Basel.

Chapter 8

46   P. Trachsel, *Tourismus und Verkehr*, unpublished, Bern, 1977.
47   T. Chorherr, *op. cit.*, p. 45.
48   Der Spiegel, *Stress im Urlaub, op. cit.*
49   *Ibid.*
50   J. Habermas, quoted by: R. Bleistein, *Freizeit ohne Langeweile* (Freiburg i. Br.: Verlag Herder, 1982), p. 140.

51 R. Bleistein, *Freizeit ohne Langeweile, op. cit.*, p. 140.
52 T. Chorherr, *op cit.*, p. 43.
53 Studienkreis für Tourismus (ed.), *Urlaubsreisen 1986, op. cit.*, p. 68.
54 *Ibid.*, p. 67.
55 P. Rieger, *Glücklicher Urlaub . . ., op. cit.*, p. 21.
56 P. Rieger, *Glück im Urlaub*, unpublished, München, 1983, p. 10.
57 R. Bleistein, *Freizeit wofür?* (Würzburg: Echter-Verlag, 1978), p. 46.
58 Quoted by: Terramar GmbH (ed.), *Länderstenogramm Peru* (Frankfurt: Terramar, n.d.), p. 14.
59 J. W. v. Goethe, quoted by: H. Niederer, Reisen – eine lehrbare Kunst? *Vorarbeiten für eine künftige Pädagogik des Reisens* (Tübingen: Universität Tübingen, 1977), p. 63.

Chapter 9

60 J. Osborne, Insult them and they may go away. In: *Evening Standard*, 28/7/1978, p. 19.
61 Quoted by: *Der Fremdenverkehr*, No. 1/1979, Darmstadt. pp. 48–50.
62 Quoted by: Booklet Pro Erschmatt, *Verein zur Förderung touristischer und nicht-touristischer Entwicklungsmöglichkeiten*, Erschmatt, n.d.
63 H. Elsasser, H. Leibundgut, M. Lendi, H. Schwarz, *Nicht-touristische Entwicklungsmöglichkeiten im Berggebiet* (Zürich: Institut für Orts-, Regional- und Landesplanung an der ETHZ), 1982.
64 For example, the International Workshop on Tourism, sponsored by the Christian Conference of Asia, in Manila, 12–25 September, 1980.
65 For example, U. Mäder, Fluchthelfer Tourismus: *Wärme in der Ferne?* (Zürich: rotpunktverlag, 1982).
66 For example, the booklets of the Arbeitskreis für Tourismus und Entwicklung, Basel (for example, *Nepal und seine Touristen*, Basel, 1983).
67 Ecumenical Coalition on Third World Tourism (ed.), *Contours – Concern for Tourism*, Bangkok.
68 Quoted by: *Welt am Sonntag*, 6/6/1982, Hamburg.
69 Quoted by: *Die Welt*, No. 150/1982, Bonn.

Part Three: For a Humanization of Everyday Life

M. Tournier, Ferien als Entwurzelung. In: *Brückenbauer*, No. 32/1980, Zürich, p. 7.

Chapter 10

1 H. Hoffmann, *Kultur für alle. Perspektiven und Modelle* (Frankfurt: Fischer Taschenbuch Verlag, 1981), p. 366.
2 H. W. Opaschowski, *Probleme im Umgang mit der Freizeit* (Hamburg: B.A.T. Freizeit-Forschungsinstitut, 1980), p. 7.

3   *Ibid.*, p. 6.
4   H. W. Prahl, *Freizeit-Soziologie. Entwicklungen – Perspektiven – Konzepte* (München: Kösch-Verlag, 1977), p. 44. SBG-Wirtschaftsnotizen, No. 5/1983, Zürich, p. 10.
5   C. D. Frechtling, Leisure Trends and Tourism Management. In: *Leisure – Recreation – Tourism*, AIEST (ed.) (Bern: Editions AIEST, 1981), p. 107.
6   *Statistisches Jahrbuch der Schweiz*, several issues. *Statistisches Jahrbuch für die Bundesrepublik Deutschland*, several issues.
7   E. Noelle-Neumann, Freude, Freiheitsgefühl und Produktivität. In: *Frankfurter Allgemeine Zeitung*, No. 111/1983, p. 13.
8   *Ibid.*, p. 13.
9   Analysis Erickson/Marplan-Institut, quoted by: Deutsches Institut für Wirtschaftsforschung, *Internationale Tourismus-Daten und Analysen* (Berlin: Ausstellungs-Messe-Kongress GmbH, 1983), p. 13.
10 Investigation by Isopublic, *Le Suisse et le travail* (Zürich: Institut für Markt-und Meinungsforschung, 1982), p. 16.
11 Arbeit 81 – Absichten und Erwartungen der Arbeitnehmerschaft der deutschen Schweiz. In: *IPSO aktuell*, No. 1/1981, Zürich, p. 9.
12 H. W. Opaschowski, Freizeit: Zur Langeweile verurteilt? In: *Animation*, No. 1/1983, Hannover, p. 2.
13 *Der Spiegel*, No. 49/1982, Hamburg, p. 34.
14 R. Kaiser (ed.), *Global 2000, op. cit.*, p. 42.
15 A. Peccei. In: *Schweizerische Handelszeitung*, No. 38/1982, Zürich, pp. 5/10.
    OECD (ed.), Analysen und Prognosen der OECD zur Arbeitslosigkeit. In: *Neue Zürcher Zeitung*, No. 222/1983, Zürich, p. 21.
16 Quoted by: *Der Spiegel*, No. 5/1982, Hamburg, p. 127.
17 Analysis by Siemens, quoted by: *Der Spiegel*, No. 49/1982, Hamburg, p. 37.
18 Quoted by: *Der Spiegel*, No. 49/1982, Hamburg, p. 37.
19 R. Dahrendorf, Die Arbeitsgesellschaft ist am Ende. In: *Die Zeit*, No. 48/1982, Hamburg, p. 44.
20 Quoted by: *Der Spiegel*, No. 49/1982, Hamburg, pp. 34–5, and *Der Bund*, No. 279/1982, Bern, p. 2.
21 P. Bichsel, quoted by: *Animation im Siedlungsbereich – a conference report* (Zürich: Pro Juventute, 1981), p. 7.
22 Eidgenössische Kommission für die schweizerische Gesamtverkehrskonzeption (ed.), *Der Freizeit- und Ferienverkehr in der Schweiz* (Bern, EDMZ, 1977), pp. 35–7.

Chapter 11

23 Quoted by: bilanz, *Schweizer Wirtschaftsrevue*, No. 2/1982, Zürich, pp. 48–50.
24 H. W. Opaschowski, G. Raddatz, *Freizeit im Wertewandel* (Hamburg: B.A.T. Freizeit-Forschungsinstitut, 1982), p. 34.

25 H. W. Opaschowski, Freizeit verändert den Alltag. In: *Animation*, No. 12/1982, Hannover, p. 421.

26 H. W. Opaschowski, Freizeit im Wertewandel. In: *Animation*, No. 8/1982, Hannover, p. 306.

27 H. W. Opaschowski, *Freizeit verändert den Alltag, op. cit.*, pp. 421–4.

28 Quoted by: *Werbung – Publicité*, No. 1/1982, Zürich, p. 6.

29 Quoted by: *Der Spiegel*, No. 42/1982, Hamburg, p. 20.

30 H. C. Binswanger, W. Geissberger, T. Ginsburg, *op. cit.*, pp. 29–32.

31 J. Huber, *Die verlorene Unschuld der Oekologie* (Frankfurt a. M.: S. Fischer Verlag GmbH, 1982), pp. 156–7.

32 H. W. Opaschowski, Freizeit im ökonomischen und sozialen Wandel. In: *Wirtschaftskunde*, No. 6/1982, Hamburg, pp. 2–5.

33 K. Röhring, quoted by: E. Eppler, *Wege aus der Gefahr* (Hamburg: Rowohlt Verlag GmbH, 1981), p. 219.

34 Opinion poll by B.A.T. In: H. W. Opaschowski, G. Raddatz, *op. cit.*, p. 16. Opinion poll by Infratest. In: *Der Spiegel*, No. 29/1983, Hamburg, p. 66. Opinion poll by ISOPUBLIC. In: *Schweizerische Handelszeitung*, No. 22/1983, Zürich, pp. 3–4.

35 Teriet, Mit mehr Zeitsouveränität zu einer neuen Arbeitszeitökonomie und zu einer grösseren Arbeitszeitflexibilität. In: *Arbeit – Beispiele für die Humanisierung*, Gottlieb Duttweiler Institut (ed.) (Olten: Walter-Verlag, 1983), pp. 81–2.

36 A. Gorz, *Wege ins Paradies* (Les Chemins du paradis) (Berlin: Rotbuch Verlag, 1983). G. Adler-Karlssohn, N. Meyer. In: *Der Bund*, No. 279/1982, Bern, p. 2.

37 B. Russell, *In Praise of Idleness and Other Essays* (London: George Allen & Unwin Publishers Ltd., 1976), pp. 15 and 23.

38 J. Huber (ed.), *Anders arbeiten, anders wirtschaften* (Frankfurt: Fischer Taschenbuch Verlag, 1979), p. 24.

39 M. Weiss, P. Lanz (eds.), *Handbuch für Quartier-Verbesserer* (Zürich: Ex Libris Verlag, 1980).

40 Zürcher Arbeitsgruppe für Städtebau, *Freiräume – Toleranzräume* (Zürich: ZAS, 1981).

41 W. Fritschi, *Freizeit in Luzern* (Luzern: Beratungsdienst Jugend Gesellschaft, Mühlenplatz 5, CH-6004 Luzern, 1981).

Part Four: Proposals for the Humanization of Travel

A. Imfeld, Tourismus hinterfragt. In: *Ferntourismus und Entwicklung*, Gottlieb Duttweiler-Institut (ed.) (Zürich: Gottlieb Duttweiler-Institut, 1979), p. 18.

Chapter 12

1 See note 11 (Part One).

2 H. Niederer, *op cit.*, p. 149.

3   *Ibid.*, p. 150.
4   J. Krippendorf, *Die Landschaftsfresser* (Bern/Stuttgart: Hallwag Verlag, 1975), p. 86.
     Beratende Kommission für Fremdenverkehr des Bundesrates, *Das Schweizerische Tourismuskonzept, op. cit.*, p. 58.
5   B. Joerges, D. Karsten, *Tourismus und Kulturwandel, op. cit.*, p. 9.
6   H. Hoffmann, *Kultur für alle, op. cit.*, p. 357.
7   O. Höffe, Wirtschaftsordnung und Gerechtigkeit. In: *Sittlich-politische Diskurse* (Frankfurt: Suhrkamp Verlag, 1981), p. 111.
8   R. Schober, Die räumliche Animation. In: *Animation*, No. 1/1980, Hannover, p. 24.
9   W. von Redack, Menschlich, anders, originell? In: *Der Fremdenverkehr*, No. 4/1983, Darmstadt, p. 2.
10   H. W. Prahl, A. Steinecke, *Der Millionen-Urlaub* (Darmstadt: Hermann Luchterhand Verlag, 1979), p. 10.
11   *Ibid.*, p. 256.
12   Les Karellis (Savoie), Val Louron (Pyrenées), Montclar (South Alps), Basse Casamance (Senegal).
13   J. Bugnicourt, *op. cit.*, p. 33 and R. O'Grady, *Third World Stopover*, The tourism debate (Geneva: World Council of Churches, 1981), p. 53.

Chapter 13

14   J. Krippendorf, *Fehlentwicklungen* . . ., *op. cit.*, pp. 55–8.
15   P. Lainé, *op. cit.*, pp. 128–35.
16   B. Bornet, Meine touristische Lageanalyse ist optimistischer. In: *Schweizer Tourismus – Weichen für die Zukunft richtig gestellt? Op. cit.*, pp. 69–75.
17   H. Weiss, *Die friedliche Zerstörung der Landschaft* (Zürich: Orell Füssli Verlag, 1981), p. 182.
18   See note 12 (Part IV).
19   J. Krippendorf, *Fehlentwicklungen* . . ., *op. cit.*, pp. 55–8.

Chapter 14

20   R. O'Grady, *Third World Stopover, op. cit.*, pp. 50–3.
21   H. M. Müllenmeister, H. Waschulewski, Animationsmodell Länderkunde. In: *Mehr Ferienqualität, Studienkreis für Tourismus* (ed.) (Starnberg: Studienkreis für Tourismus e. V., 1978), pp. 225–53.
22   D. Kramer, Die Krise des Massentourismus. In: *Wandern und Bergsteigen*, Stuttgart, 2/1979, pp. 3–6.
23   R. O'Grady, *Third World Stopover, op. cit.*, pp. 60–1.
24   Aktion Dritte Welt (ed.), 'Klar, schön war's, aber . . .', *Tourismus in die Dritte Welt* (Freiburg i. Brsg.: Aktion Dritte Welt, 1983), p. 139.

Chapter 15

25 R. Bleistein, *Freizeit ohne Langeweile, op. cit.*, pp. 85–6.
26 R. O'Grady, *Third World Stopover, op. cit.*, pp. 64–5.
27 H. R. Müller, Masaitänze pünktlich um drei. In: *Uni Press*, No. 40/1983, Bern, p. 33.

Chapter 16

28 K. Finger, B. Gayler, H. Hahn, K. D. Hartmann, *op. cit.*
29 Quoted by: H. W. Liebheit, Club Aldiana, Manchmal nervt der ganze Trubel. In: *Restaurant und Hotel Management*, No. 9/1983, Hamburg, p. 54.
30 H. W. Opaschowski, *Allein in der Freizeit* (Hamburg: B.A.T. Freizeit-forschungsinstitut, 1981), p. 26.
31 P. Fuhrimann. In: *Basler Magazin*, No. 38/1982, p. 3.
32 P. Lainé, *op. cit.*, pp. 179–81.
33 H. W. Opaschowski, G. Raddatz, *op. cit.*, pp. 42–3.
34 Studienkreis für Tourismus e. V. (ed.), *'Sympathie-Magazine'* for several countries.
35 Institut für Film und Bild in Wissenschaft und Unterricht, films 'Blickwechsel' about holidays in several countries in the Third World.

Index